Youth Crime
and Urban Policy

A Conference Sponsored by the
American Institute for Public Policy Research

T0266208

Youth Crime and Urban Policy

A View from the Inner City

Edited by Robert L. Woodson

American Enterprise Institute for Public Policy Research
Washington and London

This conference and publication were made possible by grants from the Rockefeller Brothers Fund and the Charles Stewart Mott Foundation. Special appreciation goes to the Grassroots Network members who gave generously of their time and knowledge, and to Ruth Ericson and Anne Miller for their editorial assistance in preparing this volume for publication.

Library of Congress Cataloging in Publication Data
Main entry under title:

(AEI symposia ; 81D)
Proceedings of a conference sponsored by the American Enterprise Institute and held in Washington, May 1980.
Includes bibliographical references.
1. Juvenile delinquency—United States—Congresses. 2. Urban policy—United States—Congresses. 3. Youth—Government policy—United States—Congresses. I. Woodson, Robert L. II. American Enterprise Institute for Public Policy Research. III. Series.
HV9104.Y684   364.3'6'0973   81-3459
ISBN 0-8447-2209-X   AACR2
ISBN 0-8447-2210-3 (pbk.)

AEI Symposia 81D

Participants

John (Flint) Agosto
The Ching-A-Ling Community Development Corporation
Bronx, New York

Robert Aguayo
El Centro del Pueblo Community Center
Los Angeles, California

Robert (Fat Rob) Allen
The House of Umoja
Philadelphia, Pennsylvania

George Amos
South Arsenal Neighborhood Development Corporation
Hartford, Connecticut

William J. Baroody, Jr.
American Enterprise Institute
Washington, D.C.

Brigitte Berger
Smith College
Northampton, Massachusetts

Peter Berger
Boston College
Boston, Massachusetts

Irma Torres Colon
Dispensario San Antonio, Inc.
Ponce, Puerto Rico

Nizam Fatah
Inner City Roundtable of Youth
New York, New York

David Fattah
The House of Umoja
Philadelphia, Pennsylvania

Sister Falaka Fattah
The House of Umoja
Philadelphia, Pennsylvania

Sister M. Isolina Ferré
Dispensario San Antonio, Inc.
Ponce, Puerto Rico

Lewis Fields
Youth in Action
Chester, Pennsylvania

Patricia Fountain
Youth in Action
Chester, Pennsylvania

Wilma Garcia
The Ching-A-Ling Community Development Corporation
Bronx, New York

V. G. Guinses
SEY YES, Inc—Youth Enterprise Society, Inc.
Los Angeles, California

Carl Hardrick
South Arsenal Neighborhood Development Corporation
Hartford, Connecticut

James Hargrove
New York City Police Department
Brooklyn, New York

Robert Hill
National Urban League
Washington, D.C.

Tommie Lee Jones
Youth in Action
Chester, Pennsylvania

Al Martin
The Youth Identity Program, Inc.
Bronx, New York

Albert (Crazy Cat) Mejias
Inner City Roundtable of Youth
New York, New York

Rose Nidiffer
El Centro del Pueblo Community Center
Los Angeles, California

Robert J. Pranger
American Enterprise Institute
Washington, D.C.

Darryl (Tee) Rodgers
SEY YES, Inc.—Youth Enterprise Society, Inc.
Los Angeles, California

Robert Selby
The House of Umoja
Philadelphia, Pennsylvania

Robert L. Woodson
American Enterprise Institute
Washington, D.C.

Jerry Wright
The Youth Identity Program, Inc.
Bronx, New York

*This conference was held
at the Mayflower Hotel in Washington, D.C.,
in May 1980*

Contents

PART TWO
THE YOUTHS' EXPERIENCES
and
YOUTH CRIME AND URBAN POLICY

Foreword

This unusual forum, sponsored by the American Enterprise Institute, brings together both scholars and nonprofessionals concerned with juvenile crime prevention. They include former gang members and other inner-city youth who through community grassroots programs are helping to make their neighborhoods safe.

This forum is part of the AEI mediating structures program, which studies the links between individuals on the one hand and political, economic, and social institutions on the other. Intermediate structures such as neighborhood groups, voluntary associations, churches, families, and ethnic subgroupings bridge the gap between individuals—who may be isolated, powerless, and lonely—and large, often impersonal structures, such as big government, big business, big social programs, and big education.

Fundamental to this program is a recognition that economic satisfaction and personal security, however important, are merely two aspects of personal well-being. If we act wisely, we can improve our personal well-being, but only if we reexamine the individual in his or her relationship to other citizens, to government, and to social problems. Individuals voluntarily working and planning together can help solve many of our most pressing public policy questions.

Despite expenditures by the federal government to upgrade our urban centers, they continue to decline. Clearly, something different is required to make our efforts effective. We must determine the mix of public policies and neighborhood strategies most likely to lead to urban revitalization. We must find new grounds for optimism in the residents of our cities and develop programs in which government plays a supporting role. These residents—individually and at times banded together—should play the primary role in preserving their own dignity and in making themselves self-sufficient.

This transcript of our forum has been edited lightly to preserve the informal, conversational nature of the discussion. We believe that the exchanges offer a valuable insight into the problems the participants have faced. And, we believe, it is an excellent way to encourage the "competition of ideas" that is AEI's trademark.

WILLIAM J. BAROODY, JR.
President
American Enterprise Institute

Introduction

ROBERT L. WOODSON

This forum, which met in May 1980 in Washington, D.C., was a convocation of nine neighborhood-based organizations that have been working effectively with troubled or delinquent youths of America's largest cities. Representatives of these urban organizations met to share their experiences and to describe their programs to counter youth crime in their own neighborhoods. The forum was unique in that it was made up entirely of nonprofessional, self-taught experts on youth problems, and included former gang members and other young people from high-crime, high-risk urban centers who had been helped by the local programs.

The American Enterprise Institute, sponsor of the youth forum through its Mediating Structures Project, has been studying these urban neighborhood groups, seeking to determine how nongovernmental projects of this kind can be successful in dealing with social problems, including the pressing problem of juvenile crime and delinquency.

In two days of round-table discussion, forum members identified three major areas of concern that they encounter in their work. They found that one set of common problems concerns their relationships with the criminal justice system and with various government agencies empowered to exercise authority over aspects of what they are doing. A related problem is the constant search for financial support from funding agencies. Forum members also explored the problems and issues in interacting with the young people who need their help. Panel members described to one another their philosophies and ideas, as well as the hard-earned experience of their programs. They sought to identify the special needs of young people who grow up on inner-city streets and to analyze their own strengths in meeting these needs. In mutual consultation, panel members endeavored to make explicit the steps they have taken to build their remarkable record of success with former gang members and other juveniles.

After two days of talks, the forum as a group strongly reaffirmed the contention that authentic solutions to social problems cannot come

1

from abstract academic discussion alone or from mere reanalysis by human services professionals and government authorities of standing practices and precedents. Instead, when social problems call for doing things to or for people with these problems, it is mandatory that the people themselves become the foremost participants in any policy established and any solutions attempted. Communities themselves must be in charge of their own revitalization and reform services.

The final act of the youth forum was to initiate by unanimous vote a united front organization to be called the Grassroots Network. All interested black, Puerto Rican, Hispanic, or other minority groups serving youth through community organizations will be encouraged to participate in the exchange of information and mutual aid through the network. Youth forum members, incorporated as the network, plan to move collectively to help guide other minority communities toward self-determination and self-sufficiency.

Background of the Youth Forum

The problems of America's inner cities have never seemed more pressing or more hopelessly complex. Persistent poverty, overcrowding, underemployment, substandard housing, and physical deterioration of inner cities are stubborn facts. Urban riots act to call public attention to these conditions again and again. For most of America, the cities have come to be seen as a kaleidoscope of social pathologies requiring increased measures of control and extensive social services for the threatened and threatening urban populations.

General public concern is especially drawn to crime. Among all of the urban ills that excite policy debates, street crime is a priority item. Since the early 1960s, the United States has been suffering a crime wave of startling proportions. The Federal Bureau of Investigation's uniform crime reports show that major violent crimes nearly tripled from 1960 to 1976. Robbery-related killings increased four or five times since the early 1960s, while three out of every hundred Americans will be a victim of a serious property crime and one out of every ten will have his home burglarized. Meanwhile, the viciousness and violence of criminal attacks have increased.[1] While uniform crime reports give only a crude measure, experts declare the increase too large and too well supported by common experience to be dismissed as mere statistical error.[2]

Crime is costly to individual victims and to society at large. It

[1] Charles E. Silberman, *Criminal Violence, Criminal Justice* (New York: Vintage Books, 1980), p. 4.
[2] Ibid., p. 6.

2

disturbs the quality of life, leaving a legacy of anger, fear, and vengeance-motivated plans to counteract it. Crime undermines the social order itself by destroying the assumptions on which it is based. In addition, where crime rates are high, the economic structure of the community is weakened, as business enterprises leave, unemployment grows, and physical deterioration increases from lack of funds and services. The revitalization of urban centers must begin with successful approaches to the crime problem.

America's response to inner-city problems has been conventionally channeled through control agencies. Law enforcement problems are the special concern of police, courts, and human services bureaucracies empowered to deal with such matters.

The effective value of institutional control and help summoned to the aid of cities is often questioned, however. We watch the costs of crime increase yearly. Our streets are not more secure; rehabilitation rehabilitates few; violent and alienated youth remain a conundrum; the poor, of course, are still with us. A crisis of public confidence has arisen as exasperating, costly, and persistent urban problems begin to appear insoluble to many people. A reluctance to send more money after resistant conditions and a preference for tougher law enforcement instead of human services are widely advocated.

In addition, as residential patterns have shifted in recent decades, concern with inner-city problems has become increasingly a concern with black and minority populations. Whatever professionals determine should be done about urban unrest is something to be done primarily to black and minority urban residents. Research measures of urban crime and other social pathologies seem to be measures of black pathologies; controls implemented or services rendered become controls on urban black crime or services to urban black clients.

The latest available statistics support this popular idea. Marvin Wolfgang's study of a Philadelphia birth cohort (1976) shows that urban street crime is overwhelmingly perpetrated by young, poor males, a large proportion of whom come from minority-group backgrounds. Nearly 75 percent of those arrested for the seven serious crimes listed in the FBI's crime index were under twenty-five years of age, and more than 40 percent were seventeen and younger. Moreover, one-third of those arrested were poor and black, while Puerto Ricans and Hispanics made up a significant proportion of the arrested who were classified as white. In addition, among chronic offenders who had committed serious crimes, two-thirds of the multiple offenders came from lower-class backgrounds and 51 percent were black. To sharpen the point even more, if multiple offenders are divided into two groups—hard-core delinquents with five or more arrests and others with two to four arrests—the hard-

3

core group is responsible for 52 percent of all offenses and 83 percent of all index crimes. Seventy-seven percent of these hard-core offenders are poor and black. While other social groups show a predicted decline in youth population, over 48 percent of all poor, black males are under fourteen, just entering the age group most associated with serious crime.[3]

As a result, when poverty, social welfare dependency, delinquency, and violent crime combine with urban rioting to remind us that solutions are elusive, it appears to many that black populations, not social conditions, are resistant to the best professional efforts for control and reform. As money is spent and authentic social work solutions fail to appear, a policy of all-out armed warfare against black urban youth may seem a reasonable and justified response.

Many kinds of programs have attempted to deter delinquents and to control juvenile crime. The creation of the juvenile court with its range of discretionary powers to dispose of cases was based on the belief that young offenders make up a special category distinct from adults, deserving special efforts to change and reform them. Various alternative treatments have been devised by human services professionals in response to the juvenile court mandate to "save the children."

However well meant these efforts have been, the record of performance remains disappointing. No clear, significant relationship has yet been discovered between any institutional youth program and the subsequent life history or criminal activity of youth treated in these programs. Whatever success there is seems to be achieved with white, middle-class status offenders, for whom the programs now appear to be more appropriate. The needs of minority youth who commit most of the serious crimes remain largely unmet. The poor, urban minority offender is usually remanded to the secure lockup, where he stays untreated and unhelped, and is finally returned to the streets, a continuing danger to himself and to his neighbors.

Meanwhile, the persistence, even escalation, of violent urban youth crime and the apparent inability of juvenile justice programs to affect this rate alarm the public more than any other urban problem. But the concern felt by professionals in the field and by the general public is nothing compared with that felt by the urban minority population whose children are or may become clients of the justice system. Because of the immediacy of the problem for them and because of the failure of juvenile authorities to help their youth, adults in urban centers across the country have begun to take matters into their own hands.

Here and there in inner-city communities, untrained residents have

---

[3] Marvin E. Wolfgang et al., *Delinquency in a Birth Cohort* (Chicago: University of Chicago Press, 1972), chaps. 2, 4–8.

come forward to offer alternatives to the crime-prone youngsters of their neighborhoods. Without publicity, professional credentials, or official endorsement, and with little or no public financial assistance, residents of urban centers have devised programs for the children of their own communities, often dramatically reversing the rates of delinquency and patterns of gang warfare saddling their communities. These grassroots activists and innovators, who live at the scene of the crime, who cannot and will not walk away from the problem, and who suffer most from the inadequacies of institutionalized controls, have mobilized their own resources and have achieved a measure of success with their intractable youth that would be envied in professional programs.

Founders of urban community youth programs are sometimes parents, but more often they are people who themselves have successfully survived the frustrations and temptations of ghetto living and the threats of minority status. They know personally what activates the struggling, violent young people in their midst. It is clear to them that the chance that a hard-core delinquent will be rescued emotionally or spiritually is greater when those who seek his rescue can authentically relate to him and he to them. Experience shows that neighborhood people are uniquely able to provide the supportive and subjectively meaningful guidance required, so that their own youth can help themselves to wholesome maturity.

Meanwhile, juvenile authorities are largely unaware of such successful local approaches to curbing youth crime. Those who are aware of these unofficial efforts remain skeptical or indifferent to them. The Justice Department's Office of Juvenile Justice and Delinquent Prevention deploys funds largely for white, middle-class youth involved in truancy or some other status offense, while the latest policy concentrates on the diversion of white, middle-class children away from incarceration and into professional rehabilitation programs. No study is funded to inventory the success of minority neighborhood programs that keep minority youth from coming into the juvenile justice system.

Community-based youth groups face other difficulties as they seek to maintain themselves and to continue their services. Blacks who live in the urban environment and deal with its tensions and complexities on a day-to-day basis are consulted about urban problems only when riots precipitate visible crises. The actual resources and strengths of black urban communities are little known beyond these streets. Moreover, while a white middle-class public has access to the press and has opportunities to express its views, inner-city minority parents in direct contact with urban realities have few outlets to be heard and even less chance to affect policy on funds available for combating urban problems. Urban crime is increasingly a concern about black youths, but black

5

parents and black community organizations are typically not consulted by professionals; nor do professionals expect to cooperate with untrained grassroots people who attack the same problems.

Accordingly, black grassroots activists begin their programs for youths in a context especially inimical to their efforts. The effects of public policy are often encountered as obstacles to what they are doing. Regulations on zoning, licensing requirements, housing standards, requirements for professional supervision of such programs, and lack of recognition and helpful cooperation from other institutions and agencies—all of these obstruct efforts. Financial aid brings with it standards of accountability for dollars spent and an inevitable degree of outside interference, often by officials who either do not understand or are unsympathetic to the work being done. No matter how successful or helpful a program may have been, getting money together to keep it going is always uncertain and is a first-priority problem. Not only do these activists suffer from the lack of recognized, accredited status, but also they find that formal regulations may be impossible to meet when they are trying to put together a home for troubled children using only what is available in the neighborhood.

Finally, the professionalization of social workers, rehabilitation counselors, and court personnel has been taken as a license by these authorities to decide many things about the lives of others without consulting them. Professional workers enjoy power without accountability to those who become clients of their services; paradoxically, local activists, solving their own youth problems, take on responsibility and accountability without authority. As a result, communication between authorities with power, and nonaccredited, responsible activists with no power is continuously frustrated.

The Need for the Youth Forum

The crime problem is real and growing. It is highly concentrated in the minority urban youth group. Moreover, among minority populations at least, youth crime is resistant to or outside of the scope of programs guided by trained human services specialists. Typically, black delinquents receive no effective help from the justice system and remain unchanged.

At the same time, because of the legacy of fear and anger that crime provokes, there is a real danger that traditional legal guarantees of individual rights may be suspended or modified in certain cases. Tougher policies toward young offenders are already advocated, even though tough policies, which may temporarily remove a delinquent from the streets, do not especially deter him from continuing criminal activity

6

once released. The escalation of punitive responses is not related to a drop in crime rates. It is clear, moreover, that inner-city minority youths will especially feel the impact of more repressive law enforcement policies, making it even less likely that these individuals will be able to solve their problems in a positive way.

In the light of these facts and policy trends, minority parents see their children being threatened from two directions. On the one hand, they see the tradition of street crime and the complex threats of urban poverty and minority status waiting to absorb their children. On the other, they witness institutional controls being selectively implemented in ways less and less responsive to the real needs of their youngsters and becoming more and more threatening, punitive, and alienating. Justice Department policies often seem to aggravate the problems they address.

Urban community leaders stress the urgency of making a stand to protect their own youths. Urban minority youths and the generations for which they will in turn be responsible are at risk. In this context, the self-help neighborhood youth programs now appearing in inner cities represent one resourceful response to this feeling of urgency, with important results. The determination and skill put into these programs have paid off in the rescue of as many human beings as the scope of the programs could reach. Neither the urgent social need for approaches especially designed to help urban minority youths, however, nor the real success of existing programs has been enough to win the recognition or public support necessary to continue and expand these important services.

The American Enterprise Institute in Washington, D.C., has been studying the needs of successful urban youth organizations for some time. The Urban Youth Forum was convened under my coordination as a second kind of response to the urgency to find effective policies to guide programs to control and prevent youth crime. This analysis revealed that the crucial contributions of these youth programs cannot be fully realized if these groups continue to work isolated from one another and outside the main institutional structure. The recognition, financial support, and cooperation necessary to make their work fully effective will only be forthcoming when the true value of these programs becomes widely known.

The forum itself, then, had several functions crucial to policy development. It not only provided opportunities for groups to learn from one another and to plan common pragmatic strategies, but it also served to focus national attention on the successful work of the groups. If communication with authorities has been a problem, publicity generated by the Washington meeting has worked to attract public and official attention to the programs, opening the way to greater understanding between urban activists and official bureaucracies whose cooperation they seek.

Finally, the forum was successful in its immediate psychological rewards to the panelists. Beyond the best hopes of forum members, the chance to explain themselves to one another was unexpectedly stimulating and supportive to people who had been stubbornly persisting without such recognition, simply learning to do what they felt had to be done as they went along. As the advantages of maintaining such mutual support became clear to all, the meeting culminated in the vote to formalize the association as the Grassroots Network, a permanent coalition to continue to work together on the common problems of black and minority communities in urban centers. This group is to be organized separately from and independently of AEI.

Part One

The Participants and Their Projects

Robert L. Woodson and William J. Baroody, Jr., American Enterprise Institute

Introductory Remarks

WILLIAM J. BAROODY, JR.

This two-day session on Youth Crime and Urban Policy: A View from the Inner City, promises to be interesting and constructive. The American Enterprise Institute is a nonpartisan, nonprofit educational and research organization that is interested in inquiry—in trying to get an understanding with the scholars and fellows and experts affiliated with us, of the many problems that plague our society. We at the American Enterprise Institute hope to contribute, through sessions like this, to some solutions to these problems. We are particularly pleased to bring together groups from the United States and Puerto Rico that have enjoyed success not only in curbing juvenile delinquency, but also in channeling the efforts of youth into positive programs for the revitalization of their neighborhoods. The leaders and some of the participants of these programs will exchange information about their groups, the things that have worked for them in solving the problems they faced. They will learn from each other, and we will learn from all of them.

This conference is part of a three-year-old project at AEI to study what we call mediating structures—the institutions that stand between massive government bureaucracy and the individual. These groups—the church, the family, the neighborhood, and ethnic and voluntary associations—were addressing social problems long before government took on that role. Over the past four decades, as government has attempted to supplement such local initiatives, all too often it has supplanted them. The mediating structures have been generally ignored, and the individual has been left to face the giant bureaucracy alone. Dr. Peter Berger, who will be with us throughout the conference, along with Richard Neuhaus, expressed this problem best in the AEI publication *To Empower People* (1977). Through their work and that of others at AEI, such as Bob Pranger and Bob Woodson, AEI has tried to encourage public policy debate on the vital role of these in-between institutions. By studying how the groups at this conference have succeeded in bridging the gap between government and the individual youths in their neighborhoods,

11

we can take that effort one step further. I want to congratulate each one of you for your achievements. Eventually we hope to see that the needs of today's and tomorrow's society are recognized and the outmoded perceptions of the past forgotten.

Introductory Remarks

ROBERT J. PRANGER

Although my title at the American Enterprise Institute is director of international programs, I have been involved in another responsibility for the past four or five years in building the AEI project on mediating structures. In 1975, Peter Berger and the Reverend Richard John Neuhaus came to the American Enterprise Institute, when the Institute's president was William J. Baroody, Sr. He was inspired by the idea presented by Berger and Neuhaus. How do we empower people to govern themselves in a society that is as large and complex and dominated by large-scale organizations as this one? In other words, how can we keep self-government alive and build on the resources of all Americans to improve our lives? It is significant that the book published by AEI in 1977 is entitled *To Empower People.* It is not a book about *the* people in an abstract way; rather, it is a book, and a project, about the way Americans actually govern themselves and find meaning in their lives. It is about people, not about abstractions. The institutions that have been the focus of our interest in this project are not abstractions; they are the institutions of everyday life—family, neighborhood, voluntary associations, churches, and ethnic subcultures. And now we have become interested in the communities of work in business and labor.

This project is an effort to address the problems of welfare in this society in the places where they are being attacked. We have brought together those struggling with these problems—the people who are on the front lines in developing new welfare programs and programs in housing, law enforcement, health, education, and welfare—to compare notes and to discuss ways in which new national domestic policies can develop from these experiences. Those of us who have lived in Washington know how difficult it is to get something new and creative started here. The Washington research community, the journalistic community, and the government community have to be brought together with people. This project is about empowering people and making their lives better and even bringing about some new thoughts to bear on our domestic policies.

The project grew from a small first phase, consisting largely of seminar discussions in New York City in 1975 and 1976. Then a three-year project, also headquartered in New York City, was funded from 1976 to 1979 by the National Endowment for the Humanities and by the American Enterprise Institute. From that project, Robert Woodson, of the National Urban League, became a resident fellow at the American Enterprise Institute and a leader in the fight to empower people. His book, on juvenile justice, is one of five books from this project, to be published by Ballinger Press, in cooperation with AEI.

Introductory Remarks

ROBERT L. WOODSON

I have known all of you individually, visited with you in your communities over the years, and seen your work firsthand, and I cannot tell you my joy in seeing you sitting here in Washington. You have much to exchange with one another and much that is useful to public policy. This represents one of the first conferences in the country convened to glean information from people who have personal experience in dealing with youth. It seems that the knowledge and information and solutions to the problems are at one end of the continuum, while the resources are directed at the other end. This is an opportunity to come together for an exchange that builds on our strengths.

I am tired of talking about what is wrong with neighborhoods, what is wrong with the American family, what is wrong with our young people. I want to know what's right with our young people—and there are a lot of things that are right with our young people. You have embodied in your experiences some of the solutions that people are spending millions and billions of dollars to find.

To review our agenda, first, each group will have an opportunity to present its programs, what it does with young people. Following that, my colleague Bob Allen will chair a session in which the young people will talk to us and to one another about their own personal experience. We want to know what kind of changes have been brought about by the programs. Why have these programs made a difference in their lives? What is the impact of these programs on the youths? How do urban youth programs determine their success? How do they know when they are reaching young people? How do they define success, and how do they interpret it in their own communities?

Then we want to talk about the elements of success, the similarities and differences among the various groups. It is amazing how many activities in different parts of the United States and Puerto Rico deal with the same themes. We want to talk about how the programs relate to the environment. Where can we turn in times of crisis? Who can we rely on? What is our relationship with the traditional criminal justice

15

system—the police, other social agencies? How can we deal with them? We want to look at some of the state policies and procedures that interfere with what we do. If we came out of this conference with some recommendations as to how the state could stop interfering, that in itself would be an admirable achievement. We know there have been problems of credentials. If you apply for a grant, people want to know how many social workers you have on staff, how many psychiatrists, what kind of psychological testing. We want information about policies and procedures and the effect they have on programs.

Last, we would like to talk about one approach to the issue of evaluating local programs. A lot of things you do in your neighborhoods lend themselves to measurement and evaluation and documentation, but you're too busy. You may not have time for evaluation—or, in some cases, interest in it—but we do. As I have been in your communities, interviewing many of you, writing about what you do, we want to talk now about this one approach that we are proposing.

Dispensario San Antonio, Inc., of La Playa de Ponce, Puerto Rico

Sister M. Isolina Ferré

The Dispensary of Saint Anthony, sponsored by private industry and under the direction of the Missionary Sisters of the Most Blessed Trinity, was founded in 1950 to provide elementary health services to a poor population locked into La Playa, the poor area of Ponce in Puerto Rico.

Since that time, the staff of the dispensary, with the help of local citizen volunteers, has added recreation, tutoring, job training, home economics, and social service programs. Our aim is to prevent juvenile delinquency by helping the community provide self-help opportunities for their neighborhood youths.

In 1968, after I had been in Brooklyn for twelve years during the gang wars, I went to Puerto Rico to stay in La Playa, in Ponce. Ponce is the second largest city in Puerto Rico. La Playa is physically—and psychologically—isolated from the rest of Ponce by a highway, the Caribbean Ocean, and two rivers. Two-thirds or more of our inhabitants are below the poverty level. There is no employment. There is alcoholism. The educational level is low. In 1976, only 13 percent of our adult population had finished high school and another 7 percent had no formal schooling. The dropout rate is high and seems to peak in the seventh grade. In 1968, when I arrived, there was a need for much more than a health center. There were many other problems: school dropouts, delinquency, and so on. The community met and decided to improve the area. In 1969, the center, which we call COS (Center of Orientation Services), became a reality. The community leaders included some religious people and civic and social leaders, along with the ones who knew of the illegal activities of the other side of the community. All these people together decided to make this center for the community. It is grounded on the basis of community action. We proposed the

17

integral development of the men and women of La Playa through a multitude of programs that we began to develop according to our needs.

The objective of the center from its beginning has been to provide a comprehensive community-based multiservice youth diversion program for the residents of the severely deprived community. The whole community had to get involved for any success. All our kids thought they were bad. The community had to get together to help take that image away. It also had to act as an agent in the mobilization of community resources in local self-help efforts and to use the experience gained in this process for replication and training. These objectives have been drawn from the needs of the local community and also because of the failure of conventional criminal justice institutions to serve juvenile offenders adequately and to prevent delinquency.

The youth diversion service component of the center comprises five different segments—advocacy, recreation, community development, education, and human services. This advocacy is a bridge between our youth and the community at large, to fight against all the structures that were pushing them down. To get an advocate, we did not go to a professional man or woman—we went to the people of the community. We trained these people so that they would be able to work with the youth. Our advocates are not professional people but are people from the community who are professional because of their experience. In almost ten years of this work, our advocates are better than many lawyers in town. They go to court. They do almost everything that a lawyer would do. The number of youngsters served by our program is variable. As an average, we serve more than 1,000 youths monthly. This number is greatly increased during the summer, when we provide a program open to all the youths of the area. Since many do not attend classes during this period, we call our program a university, the mini-university of the streets of La Playa; it is well attended and well taken care of.

While our greatest orientation is to our youth, the center serves the whole La Playa community. Consequently, the total number of persons affected by our efforts is considerably higher than that figure. We have been successful for the last eight years. We are running the health services for the whole community of La Playa, with community people administering a million dollars from a federal program. The important thing is that the community has helped. The youths are participating in this program, some as family visitors, but also in the other programs.

We have thirty-five ongoing programs. We began little; we began going to the courts, taking care of the youth affected by the courts. In 1969, for example, there were seventy juvenile delinquents found guilty by the courts. This year we only had eight cases in juvenile court. What has happened to the rest? We divert them. We go to the police station and pick them up there. The community brings them to us. We have all kinds of programs to involve them so they're not arrested and brought before the juvenile courts. Those eight juvenile cases were given back to us, not sent to institutions. It is very seldom we cannot take care of a kid.

Our idea is that the home gets involved. We not only have advocates to work with the kids, but we also have family advocates, a new concept that we started. The family advocate is a whole family trying to help other families in crisis in the same neighborhood. La Playa has twenty barrios (a barrio consists of about four streets). They are significant, those barrios. Before, one barrio did not talk to another. There were fights between them. Now we are all together in one effort to make a community unite. We got the barrios together through baseball games, basketball games, big fiestas. The community began to unite as a whole. We have 18,000 or 20,000 people together as La Playa, not twenty barrios.

We also have a program for girls. One of our big problems was the girls. In Puerto Rico, society always puts women second, despite the feminist movement. We have to accept the man as the head of the family. Women are not allowed out alone after they are twelve years old. Of course, they rebel, and that's where they are—out in the streets at twelve years old. As a result, we have a lot of pregnancy, we have a lot of running around. We started a new program for girls in which we try to socialize them before twelve years of age.

We also have a photography program. The project has given dignity and respect to our youth; before, they had never succeeded in anything. We started because somebody gave us some cameras—imagine, giving poor people cameras. We took a bathroom and used it as a darkroom. From that little bathroom-darkroom, we have developed the most beautiful photography program in Puerto Rico. Not only that, we put out a calendar every year, with pictures documenting the life of La Playa; these are taken by kids from twelve to sixteen or eighteen. Our pictures were so beautiful that they were exhibited in the Metropolitan Museum of New York. They have gone all over the States and London and Scotland. We have given respect and dignity to our people. Every kid in that program is a success. They are the successful kids that do the calendar known throughout Puerto Rico and the mainland. This is one success story. We have many other success stories.

When the kids are given to us from the court, we can't say to them, "Be good and go home." We have to give them work. The Comprehensive Employment and Training Act (CETA) gives us certain jobs. There are many unemployed kids, and there is no regular employment. Our rate of unemployment in La Playa is 30 percent for the adults. What

19

are we going to do with kids? We decided to go into business. Since our business is in La Playa, this means we must use the sun. We had never planted anything; we decided to work with the agricultural department and plant coffee. The kids had never planted coffee in their life, but we learned to plant coffee. Today we have an enterprise with 30,000 little coffee plants, which we sell to the government. This is not only a business venture but also a training program for our kids, to learn to go back to the land. From coffee, we are going into citrus fruits and ornamental plants. We also send our people to tend gardens. The other day we charged $1,000 to tend a whole garden. When you get youngsters to have a competence, they begin to like economic development. This is where we're going. The artisan program that mixes ceramics, silk-screening, Christmas cards, and the calendar is beginning to take off. We need a business person to sell our products competitively.

We have a community board of directors, composed of people from the community and people who help us. The decisions are made by the board of directors, with input from the coordinators and the center directors. Our people are the community. Although I am a Catholic sister, I believe in the development of everybody. We are all brothers and sisters. We are all together in this, whether we're Catholics, non-Catholics, or non-Christians. We're working together. These decisions are made for the good of our community. The day-to-day running of the center is in the hands of the executive director, myself, but a person from the community is a coordinator at each location. They run the centers, and they're beautifully run. We have little shacks or little rooms or little garages where we locate our centers, and we have the four acres of land on which we grow coffee and other things.

We work not just with youth, but with everything that a community needs. We found that there were many handicapped people; they were institutionalized and nobody cared for them. That concerns delinquency, because a handicapped person in the home puts a strain on the family. Therefore we began to plan a community endeavor to help the handicapped. We wanted the parents of the handicapped and the community to accept them. Now, in our pilot project, the handicapped children are taken care of by their mothers. We show the mothers how to take care of them; the family advocates work with them at home.

Where do we get financial support? A private enterprise started us. Later, we got federal money from the Law Enforcement Assistance Administration (LEAA); this is now almost cut out. We got city money. Two years ago, the state legislature decided that we should get some money. Of course, the community helps itself and some foundations have helped.

Statistically, the center has been quite instrumental in lowering juvenile delinquency in La Playa. In 1969, this part of the city accounted for 18.7 percent of all juvenile delinquents in the municipality of Ponce. In 1970, this dropped dramatically to 15.3 percent. The successive years have shown a steady decline in juvenile delinquency. In 1979, the percentage was down to 11.5. In the short span of ten years, the delinquency rate among juveniles has dropped 7.2 percentage points. These are just numbers. We feel that the community has greatly improved. We are a community to be respected, a community that works together to help each other. If there's a problem in the community—health or social or whatever—we are there. In this sector of the community, there are no other agencies. All the government agencies are in downtown Ponce. We take care of all of the community.

We have a big dropout rate from school. We try to put the kids back to school; in a week they are out again. The administrators said the kids from the center are no good, out they go. We have an awful fight with the educational people. Therefore we have an alternative to the formal education system. We have all kinds of alternatives to keep our kids busy and also give them the basic education to be able to go places. Last week thirty-five of our youngsters passed their high school tests and graduated from high school; forty more passed ninth grade.

Robert (Fat Rob) Allen,   Ruth W. Ericson, sociologist
House of Umoja

Tommie Lee Jones, Youth in Action   Darryl (Tee) Rodgers, SEY YES, Inc.

SEY YES, Inc.—Youth Enterprise Society, Inc.

V. G. GUINSES

The gang problem in Los Angeles involves a small percentage of youth, compared with the number of youngsters who have tried to do something positive. I really don't know how I got started working on it, and I sometimes wonder why I'm still in this. When you're living in a minority neighborhood, you first must look at the need and the survival of your own kids, as well as your own relatives and friends; that sometimes puts you on the spot. One of the main reasons why SEY YES was created in 1968 was the unemployment problem. We didn't have a big name, a well-known boxer or football player or basketball player to attract members, and since most people think that if you don't have a great degree, you can't spell or read well, we decided to come up with a name that would get a second look. We took the *say* and spelled it *sey* instead. We turned the *yes* around to *YES,* which stands for Youth Enterprises Society. We left it like that because we wanted the employees, once they met the young people, to say yes, not no, about jobs. When we started, everyone thought we couldn't spell, putting *sey* for *say*. But this is how we got that second look. In Los Angeles, if you don't have a name for the spotlight, you don't get any recognition.

As Los Angeles kept growing, it kept getting a reputation for gang problems. In the black and brown neighborhood, two or three youngsters walking down the street are seen as a gang. In a well-known white neighborhood, they're a demonstration. It took five or six years for us to come up with the actual sociological behavior of gangs. Los Angeles spends a billion dollars on gang problems and comes up with no answers. Most of my young people have been with me almost nine years, without showing the bad behavior of what sociology calls gangs.

There was no money in our program for females. You know that if you go to a party, usually if a fight breaks out, it is caused by a female. Usually, if men break up a fight, the women cause that, too—"Come on, honey, don't get in trouble." So we came up with the idea of the

23

"V.G. Angels," a program for females to supplement our work with young men. I have yet to put my hand on a youngster or to cuss at one in twelve years. I have yet to go out and recruit a youngster. My angels identify the youngsters who want to do something positive. They identify the gang members who want a peace treaty. They identify the young people, especially in the inner-city school system, who need help. We work closely with twenty-five gang groups in Los Angeles County—both blacks and browns. The biggest group has 8,000 members. We provide technical assistance for every agency in Los Angeles. We work with 200 schools, with over 100,000 people.

I'm not saying we did a great job; I'm not saying I'm an expert. The kids we work with are experts. They are trained. There are only five adults on the payroll; all the rest are young people on salary. I believe in bringing the money back into the community through the young people. They may not be gang members or gang leaders, but they are respected by the gang members. To rehabilitate a youngster, you must start from the bottom.

We wanted to start our community self-help roots from basics. We wanted to recruit the parents. We started twelve years ago, but we've only been funded one year. Volunteers make up 90 percent of our program, and that is what makes it so strong. Those same people who worked with me in the beginning are still working with me. We do not hire someone because he is recommended by some politician. We would prefer a youngster who has our own degree, what we call a master's degree of street knowledge. If a kid has this degree, we want him. If the parents have a master's degree in street knowledge, we want them. This is the knowledge we have worked with and built our program with. I am not knocking other degrees, because they are valuable, too. With both degrees, we can meet our problem. We also transfer our skills to teachers and parents; we cannot be all over Los Angeles County. L.A. has one of the top gang problems in the nation. We have had no gang incident in my area in L.A. in the past two years. There have been no homicides in the schools where I worked. That rate would be good for any baseball team, batting 1000. Once we train street experts in skills, we will have solutions, long-range solutions.

We got parents, who do not attend PTA meetings and whatnot in schools, involved because lots of them will come out to see their youngsters doing something positive. They are proud of their youngsters. We must start someplace, and we start at the elementary school level.

Our crisis team is one of our most important things. We try to move on any fist fights or any arguments. If a young guy says he's going to go and jump on V.G., we want to be on top of it. If a young guy decides to hit some youngster, we want to be on top of it. My team knows how to read graffiti. In Los Angeles, the gangs advertise by graffiti. They'll put a kid's name up as a contract; we can go on to any school or community and say immediately who's there, what they're doing, where they're going, who's a "want to be," and who's a "hook." (They're not really gang members, but they want to be.)

Los Angeles spends so much money because it spends so much time on youngsters who are hooks and not real gang members. The hooks were going to jail, and the real gang members were sitting back and giving orders. Our job was to identify who were hooks and who were not hooks. When we go into a community, we work with the real leaders behind closed doors.

It's important to know graffiti in L.A. gangs. L.A. gangs write a whole history. Just about every corner has a gang identity. You may walk into one group, say F 13. That stands for the thirteenth alphabetical letter, M, which means marijuana. That tells us that when we go into that gang structure, we are dealing with a group that's not only dealing with gangs but a hard core of drugs. You may spot a group whose graffiti say "mad V.G." That tells you that that group is ready to take care of anything that comes into that neighborhood. So it's of the utmost importance to know graffiti in L.A. gang systems. I wouldn't advise anyone to go there unless he can read graffiti. Our crisis team must know how to read graffiti out there to be able to provide any type of service. Once we know what's out there, we know what to do, we know how we can deal, and we know who we can deal with.

Some of these youngsters have godparents. The kids protect these godparents, and the gang godparents get them out of jail and whatever. No one touches the godparents.

In Los Angeles, they don't believe in using their fists anymore. They believe in using their fingers—what they call in gang language, *roscoes* (guns). We had the highest homicide rate in 1974. If a kid has enough heart (courage) to pull a trigger, then they say he has heart. If he doesn't have enough heart to pull a trigger, they say he's teasing. So we also have to learn their street language, which we introduced to the state of California school system.

Also, we tell the youngsters to learn to read to survive. We create jobs for young people. Most of our youngsters do not have the best education. Therefore, when a youngster walks into my office, I ask him what he feels he can do. From that, we create a job for that youngster. We want a program where the politician, the community, the gangs, the parents, and everyone can see something positive in a youngster, where he can utilize his expertise and not be labeled as just a gang member.

SEY YES, INC.

We are the oldest organization in Los Angeles County to work with the gangs. We give recognition to the youngsters, and the pride is there. Every youngster in our program, in our community, feels he is number one; the V.G. Angels definitely feel they are number one. They don't feel anyone can do the job any better than they can.

El Centro del Pueblo

ROSE NIDIFFER AND ROBERT AGUAYO

ROSE NIDIFFER: We are located in Echo Park, which is on the west side of Los Angeles. El Centro del Pueblo developed from the Echo Park diversion project, begun in 1971 to provide an alternative to incarceration for first- and second-time offenders. Located in the inner city, the concept of the Echo Park diversion program was a prison without walls. The program was funded by the Office of Criminal Justice Planning in the amount of $150,000 anually. But the line staff, the youth counselors, refused to cooperate with the local law enforcement office by turning over confidential client information, so the program lost its funding in 1976. From this program grew El Centro del Pueblo. The community residents got together and decided to continue services for the people in the community. The twelve staff members stayed on and did fund-raising and volunteer work to keep the center open. For two years, we operated without any formal funding. Later we joined a coalition to provide a community anticrime program funded through the Law Enforcement Assistance Administration (LEAA). Now we receive a grant of $30,000 a year.

We are still in the inner city, still in the same location, but we've grown to encompass a variety of services. The main thrust, however, has continued to be juvenile delinquency prevention and alternatives for hard-to-reach youth. Some of the services that we provide are emergency assistance, delinquency prevention through recreational therapy, arts and crafts, ethnic and cultural pride classes, and trips and outings for our youth and also our younger children from eight to thirteen years old. We have summer youth employment opportunities for up to 150 economically disadvantaged youths from the ages of fourteen to twenty-one. We provide information, referral, and advocacy; we take community surveys to find out what the real needs of the community are, so the people have some input into our program. We do gang crisis intervention, gang truce meetings, gang and youth sensitivity training for the Los Angeles Unified School District and other agencies. Last year, we were able to serve over 3,000 youths, families, and senior

27

citizens through our various programs, well over our expectations. We are able to provide a variety of services, not because we are recognized by the funding sources, or local government, but because we know how to hustle. We use every opportunity to advance our program. We have staff placed at our agency from the Lutheran Social Services, CETA, LEAA, SEY YES, United Community Efforts, the Mexican-American Opportunity Foundation, and countless volunteers.

What we are best known for, and least liked for by the local law enforcement, is our work with gangs. Gangs are a major segment of our community. Los Angeles estimates there are over 300 gangs in the county, with over 20,000 members. We teach individual gang members to take responsibility for their lives and for their actions. We develop an individual program for each client based on his or her needs. We bring the leadership of each gang together to interact on neutral ground. Our agency is neutral territory for all the gangs in our community. It is probably the only agency in the community where they can all gather without any trouble. We get them to interact in positive endeavors; we minimize gang violence and youth crimes and gang deaths by involving the gangs in activities that are valued by them as being better than running the streets.

It is the input that we receive from our youth and our parents and our community that makes our program responsive to the needs of the community. We have a large parents club; an active membership meets bimonthly and contributes to our program. We also have a board of directors. The main decisions on program operations and directions, however, are made by our staff in the form of a collective. The final decisions are made by the administrative staff after consideration of all the input. It is really difficult to determine success. An example of the impact our program has had on the youths is the return of a number of parolees from the California Youth Authority to work with younger juveniles. They want to do something to help the younger kids, to keep them from going in the same bad direction that they themselves went in. We have three peer-group counselors from three major gangs in Los Angeles. They take pride in the jobs and the fact that they work at the center. At a recent dance, some members from feuding gangs came. They have had a long-standing feud going on for many years. The peer-group counselor ran immediately to shake their hands, because he was afraid of trouble. Our guy shook hands with his worst enemy. He told his home boys that this was his job, that some of these guys were co-workers, and they'd have to get along. They did; they didn't have any incidents. Later we almost had one with a guy whose nickname is Crazy. They say he earned the nickname.

Over the last four years, we have operated employment programs for over 2,000 youths both during the summer and in the school year. The program has allowed youths an opportunity to further their education with the money they make. Each youth can earn up to $525 for a nine-week period. This year it has been cut to six weeks. The youths who are dropouts or out of school we plug into trade programs, city colleges, and unsubsidized employment in the private sector. One of our greatest accomplishments was the Brothers United program. I'd like to let Robert talk about that.

ROBERT AGUAYO: I also work for El Centro del Pueblo Community Center. A few years ago, we started a group meeting called Brothers United. We've had six gangs represented in this. Each week we would meet to discuss what was happening in the area. If a fight broke out between two gangs and nobody knew what really happened, this was the time to say what happened, why it happened, that we should prevent it and how we would prevent it. It was a time for expressing feelings and resolving problems, instead of letting things go on, with someone getting killed. We had an average of sixty youths from each gang represented at each meeting, 360 people. When there are that many people in one room without fighting, that's impressive. We met for six months, constantly discussing what was happening. We appeared on CBS News, with Walter Cronkite, on a segment about gang meetings. During the filming, we almost had a big fight, because they were filming too much of one gang and the other gang did not like that.

For serious matters, three representatives from each gang met. After a shooting or a stabbing or other incident, we would not have all the gang members from each group meet, because when you have all the members from each gang, it is hard to control the situation. With three members, we could relate to these people and we could trust them. We had the three most influential persons in their neighborhoods. We found out through this work that harmful gang activity can be prevented. For our general meetings, we had people come in to discuss employment. We had policemen come in—a very few policemen; not many wanted to participate. When we had these meetings, the police would often raid them and arrest people. They were trying to prevent us from doing this. That's one of our main problems in the Los Angeles area—the police do not cooperate with us.

V. G. Guinses, SEY YES, Inc.

Rose Nidiffer,
El Centro del Pueblo
Community Center

MS. NIDIFFEF

The House of Umoja

SISTER FALAKA FATTAH

The House of Umoja is a publishing house developed from the third black power conference in 1968. That conference was attended by over 5,000 people who came from across the country, the Caribbean islands, and Africa. The black people were concerned about becoming as extinct as some of the Indian tribes if the riots continued, and no one understood the causes of the riots. I was given the job of creating a method of communication by which people could better understand black people. Since the theme of the conference was *umoja,* a Swahili word meaning unity, I called the project the House of Umoja. For the first year, we produced *Umoja* magazine, which was well accepted not only in Philadelphia but also across the country. We had established an editorial policy, however, that we were not going to present any problems to the black people for which we didn't have any solutions. When we started getting letters from all over the country asking why children in Philadelphia killed each other, I didn't have an answer. I didn't know anything about that. I didn't even know that one of my own sons was a member of a gang and the only person on the staff who had any street knowledge. Everybody knew how to sell ads and make beautiful layouts and things like that, as artists, writers, and photographers. Nobody knew what was going on out in the street except Black Dave (my husband's street name). We asked him to do some research to find out what was going on. He had a good time because he could go to the bars and hang out in the pool rooms and stay out late. He was gathering data for three months.

Meanwhile, I had been working on a book, which will probably never be finished, that dealt with the strength of black people as we had existed in Africa, before Africa was cut up. It dealt with the strength of the black family. Dave's information showed the breakdown of the family in many cases and showed the kids were imitating some of the people they had seen in the gangster shows. They were walking like that, talking like that, and doing all the things like that. Also, they were dying at a rate of about forty a year. Dave and I were sharing the same typewriter; while he described the breakdown of the family, I talked about the strength of the family. We came to believe that part of the solution might be found if we could somehow re-create an African family in the middle of the ghetto where we lived. Our chief motivation, more overwhelming than the professional motivation, was the discovery that one of our sons had joined a gang. In Philadelphia, sometimes you didn't have too much choice about that, if you were going to live. Nevertheless, we were very upset.

When we presented our findings to the editorial staff, we said that we couldn't put our conculsions in the magazine. Nobody would believe that our idea made any sense, because we had no proof. Neither one of us had any credentials as far as the world of social work is concerned, so we set out to demonstrate that this idea might work. We decided to use our own family as the experiment. We invited fifteen members of my son's gang to come to live with us. However, we couldn't continue to produce the magazine and take care of the kids too. It was physically an impossibility; so we let the magazine go. We began to devote our entire time—twenty-four hours a day, seven days a week—to our enlarged family, which was quite an experience. It is now 500 kids later. It has been a great adventure, to say the least.

When Mayor Rizzo took office, we found we couldn't just stay in our little cocoon in West Philadelphia because when he took office, he asked all the gangs to turn in their weapons. We didn't think they were going to do that and we were afraid of what might happen if they didn't. So the kids and I talked about what we should do. By this time, over 200 kids had lived at the house. We decided everybody should go back to his own corner and get the leaders of the corners to meet to discuss this. Dave was upstairs asleep during the meeting. When I told him about the proposed gang conference, he said we were crazy. It wouldn't work, and he wasn't going to have anything to do with it. But we knew he would not let us down, so we went ahead with our plans. Then about three days before the meeting, he asked who was coming. He said you can't talk to this one unless you have rivals. You've got to have so and so. He made sure that the nuts and bolts were there. We thought we were going to have a conference of about 100 people. We were surprised when 500 gang members came to the conference and checked their guns and weapons. I looked around and said maybe Dave was right—this was crazy. That was in 1972.

We had a series of conferences and some measure of success. But we wanted to have an all-out campaign to end the gang problems. We figured that the best people to help us would be the brothers in prison, since they had the most respect. We traveled to every prison in Pennsylvania where the brothers with the most respect were; we asked them to help us plan the final conference. I think this is why it was successful.

They knew what they were doing; they were the experts. We planned a whole campaign. A lot of people got involved in it, people who had never been involved before. People in every neighborhood started coming up with different youth programs. It just caught fire. Since 1974, that enthusiasm hasn't died. All kinds of church people who had not dealt with that element got involved. The city got involved, beginning a crisis intervention team in 1975. It was an explosion of love. We had thought, when we started with this experiment, we would do it for a year. Every year it just got bigger, it just kept growing. Now we're talking about developing an urban boys' town.

We already have a two-part employment program. One is for those coming out of prison, to whom we feel a debt. Whenever they come out, we try to get them to come to the house for sixty days to get themselves together. We're able to give them a job for the sixty days and test them to see what field of work they might want to go into. We tried to get the governor to give them amnesty because of their role in stopping gang warfare, but the state didn't agree with our perspective. In place of that, we have a neighborhood employment program so that the kids don't think they have to belong to a gang or go to jail to get a job. We have a security service where the brothers themselves patrol the streets and provide escort services to the elderly. We install locks in people's homes. We said, "If you live alone or if you're elderly, we'll put locks on." "Yes," they said, "and when will you come back and break in?" But it's been very successful. There haven't been any break-ins; so now more and more people want the lock service. We also install smoke detectors in people's homes for fire prevention. We guard forty businesses in our immediate area and have a contract with a new shopping mall, which we guarded during construction to prevent vandalism. There are other people who want to have a security contract with the House of Umoja. They think it's unusual that our fellows can provide security without carrying guns. Their reputation precedes them. The other part of the program is Umoja Free School. Understanding where our people came from is important in making decisions about where they're going. We're going into economic development. We think that money could be made from the security program. We're going into a painting and hauling company. We're going into a publishing company; we're going to put out the magazine again. Our boys' town is going to be 50 percent economic development and 50 percent social programs. It's all going to be right there in the same block where it all started.

In making decisions, everything at the House of Umoja is based on family. The board directors are members of the family; the board has enlarged because my six sons are married and trying to make me a grandmother. The people who work at the program are partly from the family, partly brothers who have been through the program, and partly people who have some kind of expertise we need. Now that we're going into business, we have to get technical assistance; we will be looking for advice from the businessmen whose stores we guard. We're developing an advisory business council to the board.

In terms of money, we didn't have any. The first four years we raised all of our own money. After we had the gang conferences we were *discovered*. I'm not sure whether that was good or bad. We were given money for what we had been doing free. That caused a terrible upset at the House of Umoja. When you start paying people for what they had done because they felt that they wanted to, and when you talk about timesheets and regulations, it doesn't always work well. That might have been a little more traumatic for us than the gang wars. In terms of statistical results, people say we're successful. Their criteria for success and ours I think differ. They're measuring by recidivism rates. The House of Umoja was the first group home for delinquents in Pennsylvania, and we have a low rate. We don't measure that way. We think that a person is a success if he is able to function in society, whether he has a job or not, if he respects himself, if he's able to keep a lasting personal relationship with a wife or someone acting in that capacity, if he is able to avoid police contact or not. If he can contribute to society, we see that as a measure of success. Remember, the kids are in terrible trouble; people are at war with kids. Nothing has shown us that anybody cares what really happens to them.

Inner City Roundtable of Youth (ICRY)

Nizam Fatah

ICRY program clientele is largely composed of youths regarded as program resistant, antisocial, and crime prone. Eighty percent of the youths are categorized as members of street gangs, subculture groups, or motorcycle clubs. Although clients of all ethnic groups are served, the prominent clientele is black and Hispanic males and females age twelve to twenty-five from designated poverty areas.

ICRY represents fifty-nine groups, with an accumulated membership numbering in the thousands. The leadership of these groups sit on the ICRY Roundtable board and function as directors. Most of the efforts are directed to the membership of the groups, and another 20 percent of the services are geared to accommodate unaffiliated clients referred by law enforcement agencies, schools, and social service agencies. The services include: client and family counseling, positive placement analysis and referral, crime-prevention projects, vocational training, communications and public relations, crisis intervention, and legal service liaison.

I came from the Blackstone Rangers in Chicago. I saw the power, the energy, and the misdirection of that particular organization. There are a lot of things that we can do about youth that would eventually have an impact on the country. I think I was one of the first in Chicago with a revolutionary sense of what we could do in terms of the destiny of this country, how we could make it live up to its advertisements—freedom, justice for all, that type of thing. Well, Mayor Daley decided that I should leave town, and I did. I went to New York; I was working, earning about twenty-nine grand, and I had never made that much without going to prison for it. I didn't like the job; it was a ripoff program. That bothered me, so I decided to quit. The lawyer asked what I would do in terms of community development if I did quit. I said I'd either work with the women or the youth because I think that this is the only viable way to carry this country forward. I couldn't work with women because everybody would think I had ulterior motives, so I decided on youth. The lawyer said he had 200 grand, if I wanted to try it. I didn't know that 200 grand wasn't a lot of money, spread out over two years.

I started, and I became very independent. I rounded up some brothers and sisters that I knew from the Ching-A-Ling Corporation, from 5 Percent, and from various other groups. I told them we'd try to put together an organization and see whether it would work. I knew what energy there was, and what influence we had already in the neighborhood. I decided that we should try to make the youths a viable part of the program. Foolishly, I put myself in a position to be fired by two separate boards—by a youth board and by a what we call our established board. We have two boards that are set up much like Congress—a senate and a house of representatives. It took a long time to incorporate this idea in New York because no one knew quite how to set up a two-board function in a nonprofit corporation, with each board having equal power to veto or approve various functions. We think our system works better than Congress—we don't have a lot of the fights, though we do have a little lobbying here and there. The youth board comprises the youth leadership; some of that leadership is adult in various ways. The leaders are the controlling factors of most of the youth from their particular clientele. The established board is the regular board that any organization has—it's functional and necessary. So far this has worked well.

We started also because we recognized in New York—and nationwide—a certain phenomenon: the program-resistant youths, youths who do not wish to belong to any program, not because they don't know about them but because they feel the programs are ineffective, frustrating, and unsuccessful for the purpose they committed themselves to. Perhaps it was because the youth themselves couldn't determine their needs, rather than someone else selecting what they needed. Young people must be able to determine themselves what their own problems are. In our organization, when a youth comes into the program, he's not immediately met with analysis or thrown into an institutionalized situation. We don't feel that because the youths have had problems or are problems, they necessarily need to see a psychiatrist. We feel the only thing wrong with them is their condition, and that they're very poor. After a while, if we find out they really are crazy, then we do send them somewhere else. That happens too. But in any event, they come in and they even select the counseling methods they might want. We feel that their very association in a sense is a counseling situation. Hanging out with various members or staff familiar with our objectives and goals, this in itself is a positive function. When they see others doing things—I hate that term *peer pressure*—people whom they respect or know, they might become participants. Practically every function—the counseling, the referrals, and the programming—is handled by the youth board.

We're in downtown Manhattan, as a citywide agency, dealing with all boroughs except Staten Island. We don't see a lot of crime there, and our money is already Hitlered—too many fronts—as it is. We have tried to concentrate on the boroughs with the largest crime rates. With the little money that we did manage to get, like some programming money from New York City's Juvenile Justice Office, we managed to set up a housing counseling unit. Most of the gangs on the youth board—thirty-one members and about twenty affiliates—are living in abandoned buildings or nowhere at all. Most of them are interested in sweat equity and housing preservation programs and wish to set up units for themselves where their groups might be able to reside legally. They may be residing there anyway, but we're trying to make it legal, fix the places up, and, at the same time, offer low-cost housing to community residents, usually their families.

We also have a legal unit. In New York youths who are twelve or thirteen years old can be tried as adults for certain felony crimes. We have a component that advocates, investigates, and determines whether or not to take a particular case. We work with the National Conference of Black Lawyers in New York. Of course, we have to take care of the ones over fifteen years of age, and we go to court for them. We don't have a diversion program, but we try to divert anyone we can to other social functions.

We have a newsletter, *Youth-at-Large,* that we put together because we were doing all this good stuff but nobody knew about it. Every now and then somebody would write a good article, but we decided to try to control our own medium. We decided to put together our little newsletter and write nice things about us. So that's what we did. We try to let people know through the newsletter what each group does. In each issue, we spotlight certain groups—what their activities have been, whether they are negative or positive. We try to be realistic. We try to mention what our goals have been. Most of the time, our resources haven't been equal to the effort, and, as a result, we haven't been able to function in a way that we wish. This is the case with practically all the veteran organizations here.

We have a job referral program that handles about 1,200–1,500 people a year; this was ridiculous. We brought it down now to only members of the Roundtable board. Now this doesn't mean that they have to be gang leaders or club leaders or anything like that. It merely means that we would like them to be influential in the community, so that they can be a perpetual source of recruitment, a perpetual source of influence, in the community, to give a sense of credibility about where we're at and where we're coming from also.

In the last nine months, it's been almost amazing. We've been placing one out of every two youths in jobs. I think at first we had too many people coming to us looking for employment. We realized they weren't just unemployed, they were unemployable, so we didn't even deal with unemployed; we just started dealing with unemployable. Then we started looking for training programs. Now we realize there were no viable training programs out there. We would send them to be trained for something when there never was a job for them in the first place. They were getting the thirty-day black-belt course for something that most people have gone to Harvard for eight years to learn; they were expected to compete in a market area after this training program.

One of our most successful and our most visible programs deals with graffiti. New York City spends $25 million a year erasing graffiti. I think that some of those artists are greater than some of the artists on Madison Avenue; Andy Warhol has been telling us how good our work is. Germany uses the kids who are in graffiti to put it on the trains; they are paid big money to do that. England is getting ready to do the same thing. Of course, New York puts them in prison for it. We decided that we had already made graffiti respectable. We had taken it from the restrooms to subways and building façades; more people had probably seen our stuff than had seen Rembrandt's and Cézanne's paintings. Since the work was so well known, we decided to take these youths' artwork and put it on tee shirts. I'm wearing one from Brooklyn; he's wearing one from Manhattan. This went over so well that we decided to go into big business. We hoped that in five or ten years we would make so much money that we could close down the welfare arm and move into an area where we might really be able to take our place in America's economic society. Every program that we try has the goal of being self-supporting. (We've found out in funding that people don't like for you to incorporate self-supporting functions, but at the same time they don't wish to support you either.)

We went to the New York Mets with five examples of New York Mets graffiti tee shirts. See that stuff on Shea Stadium? Now we're taking it off the stadium and putting it on some tee shirts. You can sell it out there, and it's all tax deductible because the money goes back into a training program to send these guys to the New York School of Visual Arts. They'll be able to get a little money for their work, and they can set up some free enterprise, getting into the private sector by silk-screening and taking orders for large corporations. (Everybody's trying to copy this; the movie *The Wiz* spent $2 million in New York taking photographs and copying the kid's stuff from the subways and never used one of the kids who did it. They hired Madison Avenue artists to copy the stuff from photographs. It was time that we started taking advantage of our own abilities.) The Mets looked at the ideas and liked all five of them. We didn't even know how much money we wanted for them; we didn't think they were going to like them. The Mets offered about $150,000. We had to check with the lawyers, to see if we could do this. Then George Steinbrenner, president of the New York Yankees, asked for some designs. Some people in Texas wanted us to design shirts. Sooner or later, the National Black Police Association will probably want some.

We have also set up a crisis intervention unit, and if we know about something through the grapevine, we'll go over to try to keep the peace. Our counseling is one on one. We may use somebody from the home group, like the president, to help a guy. We also try to incorporate all the groups. The Ching-A-Lings were able to become incorporated as the Ching-A-Ling Community Development Corporation. Some groups wanted to be known by names like the Crazy Homicide Community Development Corporation. We said that people identify you by the name—a name like that would take away some credibility. At the same time, we didn't want to take away the group's identity. That's important to minority people. It's important that we know who we are. I'm crazy about gangs because I like the sense of collective action. Unions can't even get together, but people in gangs do. We tried to figure out what a gang is, and it is really this. A gang isn't just a group that the police are after, because the police are a gang, and the boy scouts are a gang. The difference is, one is funded and one isn't. If you're funded, you're not a gang; if you're unfunded, then you are one. We decided that if we could get every group represented on the Roundtable board funded, we wouldn't be gangs anymore. We never call ourselves that anyway; we call ourselves families, in the sense of our knowing that we belong to each other. There are plenty of arguments between us, but we try to keep it in the family. We deal with program-resistant youths—youths who have been in programs and have rejected them; the ones nobody wants in their organizations or agencies because they don't look good for funding. Everybody wants model people; they want to say we had 100 kids here, and all of them with halos. We decided not to do that.

I once told a politician I had met through Andrew Young that, because we've got nonprofit tax-exempt status, we can't be involved in anything political. That's a little stupid, isn't it. Everybody's involved in everything political, but we can't be. About fifteen members of the various gangs, are thinking about running for assembly, district leadership, and so on, like they did at the House of Umoja in Philadelphia.

The mayor said, "You know, these little fools just might make it." They called and asked us how we would like to do some training on the area policy board, just a job to get us off their backs. So we said we'd think about it.

As far as our staff expertise is concerned, I'm not a brilliant person. I haven't had a lot of education. I've been to about 9 million seminars and workshops, and taken 100,000 courses and the high school equivalency that I got in prison, and that type of thing. If I'm exposed to knowledge, I'll get it. Most of the people who work with me are the same way. But at the same time, we're not crazy enough to think that's good enough. So in all of our funding proposals now, we ask for credentialization money for staff. In the past, every one of our efforts went down the drain because we had to go outside to get help. We had to go outside for professional assistance that may not have been the assistance that was particularly needed for our agency, with its holistic concept of organization. We've had to depend primarily on outside consultants until we can credentialize ourselves. We constantly upgrade our own skills and abilities; the only resolution between using paraprofessionals and professionals is that the paraprofessionals become professionals. In the drug clinics, the paraprofessional is right in what he's saying, and the professional is almost right in what he's saying. The paraprofessional looks at the professional and asks how he can tell an ex-addict anything—he hasn't been an addict. You can't expect a professional to become an addict so that he can become a total expert, but the ex-addict can perhaps become a professional. We need that type of coordinated expertise. The government says that we can't buy anything, that everything has to be leased. So we lease our consultants; we don't actually put them on staff. We bring in a fiscal management consultant, who checks us weekly to see that we're doing what we should, and, at the same time, that consultant works in depth with one of the youths. The youth will at least have a little head start maybe in accounting. That method applies to every area.

For a long time, we were isolationists. We had to be in order to establish our work in New York City, a diverse community, where you deal with every type of individual and almost every ethnic group. All of them are clannish in a sense. An integrated group has a clannishness, too; I mean, everything is an in-crowd. We decided that at some point we were going to have to deal with law enforcement agencies rather than work behind their backs. We chose James Hargrove, president of the National Black Police Association, as our champion for law enforcement in the community. We knew what the Guardians, a police organization, and the National Black Police Association were doing in terms of the black community; they were more interested in the community-based functions than they were in tanks and guns. They recognized the sociological need; they recognized that they were also a part of that need and that they hadn't escaped the system any more than we had. They were in a position through law enforcement to buffer some of the things that were happening to our youth, so we tried this. We're in the process now of trying to put together something else like this. We probably won't even get the money, but we're trying to put together a group with the youth gangs backing the Guardians and the Guardians backing the youth gangs, like a PAL (Police Athletic League), only without the baseball bats and basketballs. We feel that recreation is great, but we think that recreation is recreation. It's after you get through working.

We've been doing pretty well. We've been hanging tough. We get a lot done, but in all these programs, our greatest effort—and the greatest impact—is more psychological; we can only feel that we've done something. We know we can do a lot more. I wanted to say also that most of the people here aren't Johnnies-come-lately. They haven't come to the youth gang scene because they think that youth gangs are going to get a lot of money. These are the best—people who have been doing it for a long time. I'm afraid now that institutions that have been set up for a long time are going to get all the money that we've been working for, the same as it always has been. The established organizations will open up a youth gang wing.

Sister Falaka Fattah,
House of Umoja

Robert Aguayo, El Centro
del Pueblo, and
James Hargrove, New York
City Police Department

The Ching-A-Ling Community Development Corporation

JOHN (FLINT) AGOSTO

With commentary by Nizam Fatah

JOHN (FLINT) AGOSTO: The Ching-A-Ling Community Development Corporation was officially chartered in 1980, but the Ching-A-Ling motorcycle gang has been in existence since 1960. We were the reincarnation of a 1950s gang in New York City, a new breed, more violent than its predecessor. The gangs of the 1950s were more social. They were started in school or in some recreational activity with close ties with family and church. The gangs of the 1950s died with the introduction of heroin. In contrast, the gangs of the 1960s, the 1970s, and today learn that heroin, barbituates, and other drugs are the path to their destruction. The gangs of the 1960s were not just a passing fad—a lot of people were saying,"Close your eyes, and it will go away." These were youths who were getting a poor education because of their ethnic backgrounds, youths who were trying to escape from their poor housing conditions, youths escaping from a large family with not enough to eat and only one parent as head of the household. In the 1950s gang membership tapered off at seventeen or eighteen years of age, when members either got married or went into the armed forces, became drug addicts, or were sent to jail. In the gangs of the 1960s and today, the members get married and bring their families into a gang. The ones who served in the armed forces and participated in the undeclared war of Vietnam and were lucky enough to survive, came back to the gang. Those who are in jail come back to the gang. The gangs of the 1960s didn't go away or die; they became better and more organized, with more of an army structure and style. The 1960s youth gangs are today's adult gangs, better known as motorcycle clubs.

A study was published in 1975 by the Office of Juvenile Justice and Delinquent Prevention, conducted by Walter E. Miller. It was called "Violence by Youth Gangs and Youth Groups as a Crime in Major American Cities." The report says a survey conducted in twelve major cities used four criteria for identifying gangs as such: one, violent and criminal behavior as a major activity of group members; two, group organizers with functional role division and chain of command; three, identifiable leadership for group members in continuing or recurring interaction; four, groups identified with claims of control over communities. Eight of the twelve respondents specified that the term *gang* applied to youth or juveniles. The remaining four felt that groups containing adults could properly be designated as gangs. Motorcycle gangs often include persons in their twenties or thirties. This study, which I find very poorly done because none of the researchers interviewed gang leaders, came close to the true identification of the gang structure in the inner city, such as New York. The structures of the street gang are very organized and disciplined. They are called families rather than gangs. The ages of members range from fourteen to retirement or death.

The Ching-A-Lings in the mid-1970s found that the community youths looked upon them for leadership and guidance. These community youths, whose ages range from thirteen to seventeen and who have all sorts of problems, came to us because of our reputation in the community for taking care of each other. The forty-five members of the Ching-A-Lings in 1975 voted to accept CETA help and guidance. We began a project for the youths of our community with counseling on education, health, and housing. The organization, lacking financial aid from any government agency, launched a project without informing the public or the proper authorities. This brought problems with the law enforcement agencies of New York City. At 6:00 one morning in April 1979, New York City's finest took it upon themselves to violate every civil right in our Constitution by forceably breaking into our homes and brandishing their well-stocked arsenal. The police were unaware that we owned our building and that everyone living there had a lease. They thought we were squatters. Every member, every tenant, every child in that building was arrested. This action by the New York City Police Department brought out the community to our support. The police, without any knowledge of our program, branded the very youths they were themselves unable to keep out of trouble, youths who for two or three years had avoided conflict with the law, youths who by the force of our personality were going back to school, youths who looked to us as parents because they never before had someone to care for them or love them. The police destroyed everything they got their hands on. They destroyed the building we lived in; they destroyed the clothes on our backs by spraying them with paint; they destroyed our appliances, our motorcycles, our automobiles. We were made to live in the streets for two weeks, without any shelter. Because of the bad publicity, no city agency would help us, other than ICRY. For two months, our organization actually lived in the streets.

Now because of our reputation over the past twenty years, law enforcement agencies have us on their blacklists. Anything that goes down in the South Bronx is blamed on the Ching-A-Lings. This brings us into conflict with the police. We try hard to work with Sergeant James Hargrove of Brooklyn Street Gang Unit No. 3, New York City Police Department, and understand Sergeant Hargrove's problems. He's understaffed; his superiors don't really care what he does as long as he gets his reports in every month. I've known Jimmy Hargrove a couple of years—I know where his heart is, with the youth of our community. Through him and through ICRY, my organization has begun to get back onto its feet. Miss Garcia, who's been with our program for about three years, is an example of our work. She comes from our community. She didn't know where her future might take her or how she was going to attack her problems. We helped her through counseling and referral. Last year she graduated from high school. She took the state regional exam and was one of the top ten finalists, receiving a scholarship for four years. So we are doing a turnaround.

But the main thing is that the gangs in New York have not died. They are better organized because the leadership is adult. Most were kids when they joined, but they're still in the gang and now they're adults. Many think there's no gang problem today in New York City because the gang unit of the police department is understaffed and doesn't see it. There's a trend coming; the police department may not be aware of it. The gangs of today are no longer wearing their colors. They wear tee shirts like everyone else. This is the new trend of the 1980s. The Ching-A-Lings, being community activists, recognize this new trend for the gangs; we have already begun to work with the new groups.

NIZAM FATAH, ICRY: The Ching-A-Lings, with their notorious reputation, brought in 800 to 1,200 people to a rally for a New York judge called Cut-em loose, Bruce—Judge Bruce Wright. The police department, the justice department—everyone came. Judge Wright happens to be on our board and on theirs, too. These groups said they'd try to establish an interaction with us. The mayor's office came to observe us. A guy from the mayor's office went to a corner grocery store with me and —you know how investigators are, they're always going to try it real slick—he asks the woman there what she thought about the Ching-A-Lings. She said if they hadn't been in the neighborhood, everybody would have been hit by independents coming in, junkies and that kind of thing. In nine years, they've always seen to it that the businesses on this block have been able to operate without extortion, she said. If they weren't there, she'd leave tomorrow. That says something.

The Ching-A-Lings are now operating without any funds, just through the grace of the Trinity Church, which has allowed them a location. Probably, because of their reputation, they will not be able to obtain any substantial funding except from a private group or individual. It's important to have groups that control certain neighborhood circumstances, that the problem youths look up to. The Ford Foundation in a study released last year, said that 63 percent of all—all, not juvenile—all indexed crime in New York City is supposed to be—as Jimmy Hargrove probably would say—perpetrated by 4 percent of New York City's youths; those particular youths have been identified as belonging to gangs or as program-resistant. Consider the amount of crime in New York City—1,700-plus homicides last year; burglaries on an average of one every twenty-seven seconds; felonies, muggings, at one every three minutes—and consider that 63 percent of this is done by the 4 percent of the youths who are not even allowed in most programs in New York. If they were allowed in, they would reject the programs as ineffective and nonviable. The very fact that they have become gang members shows that they're not program-resistant. The gang in itself is a program.

The Youth Identity Program, Inc.

AL MARTIN

In 1974, in the North Bronx, a middle-class area where I live, a division of the Black Spades sprang up; it was the most notorious street gang in the city, and this was the seventeenth division. In the course of a year, they started running up to stores, beating up on people with bats or chains, the usual thing. Some of the parents called a meeting and wanted to get guns to face the Black Spades. I pulled aside two leaders of the division and told them they'd have to change. "You're nineteen and twenty years old. Where's your future?" They said that they didn't have a high school diploma, that they were unemployable, but that I was right. Through them I met other members of the Black Spades, leaders of the other divisions in the Bronx. I said, "Look, we'll have to pull this thing together with you all. What you seem to be doing is looking for an identity."

I was driving a bus then. I rented the bus and took some of the gang members for rides in the country. I gave a few of them pocket money, which they usually had gotten by stealing. They began to trust me. They adopted me and called me "Papa Spade." We began to develop a neighborhood rehabilitation program. It started working, and we did it in other parts of the Bronx.

During this time, I devoted my money to try to develop this program. I thought it was a simple thing—you get a program and you get money. We added some youth jobs the first year with a youth service organization, which is now defunct. We put thirty gang members to work. Then we thought we should be incorporated. They said yes, it'll cost you about $1,500. I said forget it. I went to Washington, D.C., to the Department of Health, Education, and Welfare. A friend of mine had a script for a play or movie dealing with gangs. We went down to HEW, and they said they really liked it, but they said they would like us to make the film in Detroit. What was I supposed to do, just say goodbye, Black Spades, and go to Detroit? That wouldn't work. HEW told us about the Law Enforcement Assistance Administration (LEAA). I met the assistant director. He told me we were doing all right. If we

47

had come in four years earlier, we would have been given tons of money. He asked if we were incorporated. He couldn't give us money because we weren't. Then I found we could be incorporated for fifty dollars. The city councilmen in my district did it for us. We put in the corporation ex-members of gangs, ex-offenders, and so on. Because of that, it took us almost a year to get incorporated.

Meanwhile, we were still living on my personal money. We went to the New York City Youth Board; it funds groups like us. The board said it didn't fund anybody working with street gangs. So we took street gangs out of our proposal; we said disadvantaged youth—same people, different title. We got a big $15,000 grant to run our program for the whole year. Meanwhile, we were still operating out of my house. The graciousness of the Edwin Gould Foundation gave us office space in a building in my community; now at least we have an office for people to come to. About that time, I read about ICRY working with street gangs. I called Nizam Fatah, and he's feeling me out and I'm feeling him out. We're both a little skeptical. He asked me to come on down for a meeting. So I went down, and we saw that both of us were on the level. He invited me to his open house. I met an ex-gang leader, now the assistant director of the Youth Identity Program, along with other members of ICRY. Alfonso K. Ford, who was going to be assistant commissioner for the New York City Department of Corrections, was there, and he asked me to stop down to his office whenever I was free. Two weeks later, we met with some of his staff and told them what we were about and where we were going. They said we did everything backwards; we developed a program that works and then asked for money. Everybody else asks for the money to do a program.

We were invited to the Adolescent Reception and Detention Center at Rikers Island. That's the prison. They asked if the community groups wanted to come in on a voluntary basis to work with the youth, and I put my hand up. Nobody else put their hand up. We volunteered to come in on weekends to begin with, to work with the youths that are locked up, in what we call youth-for-youth peer counseling. Most of these youths are from deprived backgrounds. They have poor self-esteem and lack educational and vocational skills. At Rikers Island these adolescents are forced to live in a crowded situation—the atmosphere is very tense and hostile. Our peer counselors serve as models for the kids in jail, someone to say to them that things aren't that bad and that help is available. It worked, and we were making an impact. We were asked to come three nights during the week; we accommodated them. Still, we wanted $15,000 from the New York City Youth Board.

Then the board of directors came up with a wonderful idea as an alternative to the incarceration program at the Tombs. The Tombs used to be the men's house of detention in Manhattan, before it was closed down. We brought young boys and girls in to tour the empty jail and spend brief periods of time in the cells. They heard from ex-offenders who described their own prison experiences in the tough words that the children respect. The jail tours and counseling sessions at the Tombs are without a doubt a deterrent to the often glorified life of crime. We did our thing for the Department of Corrections. Great. We started on a five-day-a-week basis at the Tombs, once again on a voluntary basis. We had school groups, community groups, and law enforcement agencies participating, not only from New York City, but also from Connecticut, New Jersey, and Long Island. I had a regular rotating shift, running these kids downtown to do this presentation and other ones out to Rikers Island to do the other presentation. Some people looked at me and said, "You know, you're burning your boys out. You've become professional volunteers." We were willing to do this, hoping to get money. We needed publicity. There were articles in the *Daily News* and in the *New York Times*. We taped an interview for "To Tell the Truth," the television show, which was successful. They contributed $1,000 to the program. But we still had no other money, we had no jobs. Finally, in 1978, our incorporation came through. We started making some moves. We went on the "Voice of America" with some of my youth. Now we've started being noticed a bit.

I was told that the Criminal Justice Coordinating Council (CJCC) had heavy bucks. I went down to CJCC, and they asked for a letter of intent. I gave them a letter of intent. We wanted funds for a family-type project, where we would house the kids coming from Rikers and do counseling. The council bought the counseling part, but said we had to get political support. I said here we go into politics again. We met with staff people from Senators Javits's and Moynihan's offices and the congressional people. We got their support and local support.

Well, I'm very glad to say after a year of fighting, we did get the grant from CJCC to do counseling on Rikers Island. But it was a more formal thing than I would ever have thought. First of all, we were told to get professionals on our staff. We had to hire an administrator, two social workers—professionals with bachelor of social work degrees. We conceded that. We drew up everything with CJCC. It was to go before the board. All of a sudden, the commissioner of the Department of Corrections was changed. The new commissioner didn't know anything about our program. We were due to go before the board in March 1979. We were put off the March schedule and moved to May. Meanwhile, we met with the board's lawyer. This guy put me over the coals, with every little nit-picking thing in the contract. The board didn't think we should start up right away. We should do it in phases—this, that, and the other thing. The board was trying to get us to say we didn't want their money. But we worked for five years to get this money; we were so close to it, we could taste it. We bowed to a few of the board's wishes. We're going to put professional staff on the board. Finally, in July 1979, the proposal was approved.

In September 1979 we implemented the program at Rikers on a full-time basis. We take ex-gang members and pay them $9,000 to do youth-to-youth peer counseling. We have four supervisors making $10,500. All these young people have no diploma. We tied into their contracts that, in order to maintain their jobs, they have to go to night school and get the equivalent of a high school diploma (GED) within one year of beginning work. We want to build from within. We've tied in with the New York Institute of Technology, on Long Island. All the young people who complete the GED will be accepted into the New York Institute of Technology in a special program. They will have a special counselor assigned to them; two professors are going to be assigned to work with us.

We stress education. We're tied with Roth Community College, with their job adequacy program; young people released from Rikers Island come into the program. If we don't have a job for them, we send them to Roth Community College or a couple of other agencies. The Youth Identity Program is also a part of a citywide coalition sponsored by Advocacy for Children.

We have an out-of-school program, where we're employing our youth in city slots. We're also part of a coalition in the Bronx, where we pick up an additional thirty-five jobs during the summer. We're working on our own in-school, out-of-school contract. We hope to implement it in September. Well, it's been a hard road, but things are getting a little easier.

I told the commissioner of corrections that brought us into the institution and made all the agreements what we do—this, that, and the other thing—and then he was fired by Mayor Koch. So a new commissioner came in. We also made agreements with the warden of the institution. The following month, he became the supervisor of wardens, and we had a new warden. So the poor little Youth Identity Program was in the Adolescent Reception Detention Center (ARDC) for only three months and had an administration change and a warden change. All these new people knew nothing about the Youth Identity Program. We were their last priority. We hoped to survive this little crisis, and finally, in March 1980, the warden gave us a letter of appreciation. Now ARDC wants us to extend our activities to all the adolescent facilities on Rikers Island, if they give us the money. We're starting to make our moves and to make our impressions. We're trying to cut down on the recidivism rate. We're trying to get youths coming out of Rikers hooked up into something, either a job, a training program, or education. What goes on in prison is a crime. If you go there, all you see are blacks and Hispanics all over the place. It's a shame.

Nizam Fatah,
Inner City Roundtable
of Youth (ICRY)

John (Flint) Agosto,
Ching-A-Ling
Community Development
Corporation

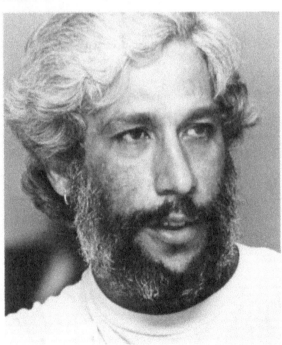

The South Arsenal Neighborhood Development Corporation (SAND)

CARL HARDRICK

The South Arsenal neighborhood is a small community, immediately adjacent to the central business district of downtown Hartford, Connecticut. It is the poorest neighborhood in the city, historically afflicted by a whole range of social and economic problems. The South Arsenal Neighborhood Development Corporation (SAND) is a community-based organization formed in 1968 to represent the interests of the South Arsenal community in dealing with these problems. SAND's membership includes blacks, Puerto Ricans, and other Latin Americans.

Under the leadership of a biracial staff and with funds from the Connecticut Department of Community Affairs and private sources, it has seen substantial victories and accomplishments in the areas of housing, education, and community service. Two hundred seventy-four units of new housing are almost completed; over three hundred public housing units are being rehabilitated; a unique alternative school has been developed within the public school system; and an innovative social service delivery system—the Neighborhood Life Center—has gotten under way.

SAND began in the 1960s, during the riots when people were being removed from a housing project in Hartford's Northside. As people were being removed by city officials, they were told that housing was going to go up, industry was going to go up; there would be a better school, a better neighborhood. As they were pushed out, they were not given the kind of assistance from the city that should have been given to them. They were just railroaded out of their houses. When they didn't move, they were told that the bulldozer was coming through, or the sheriff threatened them. They would have to move without their things, without city assistance, in violation of their rights. Industry came in; insurance companies came in; businesses came in—but no housing. The people were crowded into an area called South Arsenal. They decided that such removal was not going to happen again, in that particular neighborhood.

53

The people began to organize themselves, in the sense of trying collectively, as well as individually, to find what they could do to prevent such removal. They got some help from students. In the 1960s, students were active in communities, as attorneys, social workers, and so forth; they were utilized to the utmost. The SAND corporation started with little successes. There was a lot of police brutality at that particular time. They moved from working on the police brutality to talk about getting street lights for the area. Remember, you have to have small victories before you go to bigger ones. Youngsters were being run over or hit by cars, and the city did nothing. The people decided to do something themselves.

After they dealt with street lights, they moved to playgrounds and housing. When Hartford was having back-to-back riots in the early 1960s, the neighborhood began to negotiate with the city about doing its own urban renewal. The people were able to make some contacts within the city hall. They got information about citizen participation in urban renewal. They got grants and technical assistance from the state of Connecticut, the Department of Community Affairs, and the Community Renewal Team. They were able to learn about demonstrating and putting together a plan for housing. The people in the neighborhood started meeting to discuss their own particular problems and what the design of the housing should be. I think folks from the state said what they thought the design should be. The people said, seeing that they had to live in it, they had a better idea of what housing should be. They knew their own problems; they should know some of the solutions. SAND was able to put together a housing complex of about 682 units. The Connecticut General Insurance Company for technical assistance and an architect, Jack Darwin, at Aetna Life Insurance, gave them the design.

Because of the Nixon administration moratorium on housing, the 682 units did not go through, but they were able to salvage about 247 units. That cutback caused a lot of problems. A lot of relocated people thought that they were coming back; how do you tell 435 families that nothing's happening? How do you decide who's coming back and who shouldn't? Construction was ten years late. Construction costs shot up something like 90 percent; the project was operating almost $3 million in the red before it even got off the ground. People were getting kind of disgusted, because they weren't seeing anything but promises. In relocation, we had relied on public housing for assistance in making contact in the community with a housing project called Bellevue Square, in probably the roughest area in the city. The crime rate was high. Even the police didn't want to go into the area. You can't get a cab in that particular area. Cabs won't go there.

As SAND began to develop the 247 units there, the people started talking about a school; you cannot deal with housing without dealing with education. If we did not deal with education for the people coming into that housing, the neighborhood would continue to have the same problems. We talked about putting up an elementary school, which was to be called SAND Everywhere School. People were concerned that education should be everywhere and that the neighborhood should look like a university, because the concept of SAND was the open school, the open classroom. They felt brothers and sisters were learning more in the street than they were in the usual school. What they said was that it doesn't matter whether a youngster does his homework on a desk or on the floor, but rather how comfortable is that individual in doing his work. Accordingly, the community sought funds from the state as well as the local board of education to set up a demonstration project of 250 students from kindergarten to sixth grade in a converted warehouse. They set it up on an MIA (multi-instructional area) concept. The open-room concept was successful for the first two years; we were able to get additional money for an extended day school. Incidentally, this same concept of education was being utilized in the suburbs at that particular time. In leaving the inner city, there was an educational process in just being on the bus. Then we began to see MIA models shoot up all over Hartford. SAND had set an example for the city. In this neighborhood, as we began to move from education, we had to talk about economic development; you cannot deal with education without dealing with economics.

In meeting with people, trying to find out what were some of the things that were happening, we found that people were very afraid. There was a gang in the community, called the Magnificent Twenties, about 800 or 900 strong, and nearly everybody was terrified of them. At a mass meeting, people expressed their concerns: a fight, a shootout, a son dropping out of school. The senior citizens were afraid to go out. These were things we had to deal with, so I started working with one of the gang leaders. The summer was approaching and we had a youth work program for 200 to 300 kids. We said, if that gang issue is not settled, then the youth program will be chaotic. We were really concerned about lives; there had been a couple of shootouts. One of the brothers was working at a restaurant while the gangs were warring against each other, and somebody fired a shotgun in the window where he worked and just missed a couple of people sitting there eating. It seems not just those that were fighting—everybody else's life was in jeopardy too.

At that point, I sat down with the gangs and found they really didn't want to fight, but no one was saying, let's come together as one. We began to talk about some of the gangs' needs. We found the very thing that the brother from Los Angeles talked about—that the females were moving throughout the community and saying,"So-and-so said they were going to take you off tonight,"and the next thing you know, there would be fighting. As one began to fight, they began to bring the whole gang into the picture.

When you work with young people, you find you have to put your life on the line; you've got to be there on the front line. You cannot stand back in a church and not be out there with direct contact. That's where you earn your respect. One of the things we were able to do was to bring two gangs together, one from the Stowe Village housing project and the other from Bellevue Square. We went to the village; they said to bring the others up. There were about 400 of them, and I brought three of the representatives. One of them went home to get a gun, which I didn't realize. So we go up there to their meeting and the guys said that they were out there. They came running out there. It was a standoff; everybody stood there, looking at each other. My heart was pounding— I didn't know what was going to jump off. Someone said, "Look, you've got to be cool." They said they'd meet—any time, any place, at a neutral place. So the village gang said, they would come down to the square. Since that, we got the leaders together and we were able to get some communication where before there wasn't any. Everything had been physical; they wouldn't talk unless they talked about going to war. All you could see were 600 brothers marching up the street. It looked like an army moving in, with the cops in between, not wanting to stop it, but wanting to see what would happen.

These young brothers are our future. We had to do something to try to turn that violence around; individuals were getting stomped. They would catch one on this corner; someone would catch another on the next corner. Next thing you know, someone was in critical condition. The family gets mad, and it begins to be a family-gang kind of thing. We even had cases where there were two families in projects fighting against each other. But we were able to score ourselves, we were able to bring them together at one table. They agreed that there would be individual fights, but not gang fights. They were going to deal on a one-to-one basis.

Then we had to talk about how to deal with a particular gang, the Magnificent Twenties. People were still terrified; we talked about things they could do. Even after agreements, there were little cases of violence, but they were mostly cooled out. They would always come together and talk before they began to talk about fighting each other. That communication was the key. We talked about a neutral ground. They were able to talk about their individual differences and found out that the things they were fighting about hadn't always happened. It was just someone saying that someone was "badder" than you, that kind of thing. Rumors were bringing them to war with each other; they began to realize the seriousness of the situation.

I began to work with the Twenties, trying to organize them, realizing that there was a lot of collective movement, a lot of positive things there, but they were headed in a negative direction. I looked at the things that I thought they could do and the things that they wanted to do. They were able to work with the younger brothers, who were coming up and looking up at them. If you have a gang on this level, you also have one on the next younger level. Examples are set, and this carries straight on down to the elementary school. In the elementary school, the little brothers begin to organize themselves as gangs because those are the images they see. In contrast, we try to project positive images within the community. If the men in the community do not stand up, the brothers will do what they think should be done, which is not always the right kind of thing. The Twenties began to do some things. First, they established a couple of discos. I was trying to show them how they could make money by having people from all over come. If they policed their own business, then they wouldn't have as many problems. People could enjoy it. They invited gangs from other areas to come down, and they did. They set a rule that everyone had to check his weapons at the door, the sticks, knives, guns, everything. They put little tags on them so they could be returned. In this way they policed their own thing and everything went fine. Before, they didn't know that they could do this. There was no liquor, no swearing, no cussing, no smoking. If someone came in drunk, he had to leave and got his money back. I told them these were the kinds of things they had to enforce to have the kind of order they wanted.

Then on Halloween they gave parties for the younger brothers; they gave senior citizens turkeys, needy families turkeys; they did a lot of positive things. But they found that they weren't getting the kind of recognition that they had when there were gang wars. Articles did not show up on the front page—but on the back page of the comics, somewhere down there. They couldn't hardly find them, the articles were so small, but when they were fighting, they were on the front page. Sometimes the media becomes a contributing factor in spreading gang wars. Recently, a Hispanic gang had an incident, a murder on Park Street. The first thing on the air was that it was supposed to be the first killing of a particular gang warfare—but it didn't really happen that way. It was a family incident, where two individuals were fighting, and one got shot. They were trying to make it out as a gang incident. The youths came together and had the media correct the mistake and apologize.

You have to be careful working with youngsters. When someone sees that, if you're fighting, you're getting all the attention, then maybe he needs to be fighting too, because nobody is looking at him. He's trying to struggle, going to school. He needs help. Does he need to be in a gang to get help?

We were able to organize the Twenties. All those thinking in negative terms went away, individually; those thinking positive went on to school or into other kinds of things. We knew that with the economic stress of the times, especially the youth unemployment, we could not change the economic conditions that led to the youth and gang problems in most communities. But at least we had the expertise and spirit to get in there and do something, on the knowledge that we had—on the street knowledge—and the concern that we had—that it was not going to be done otherwise. The Twenties still exist but very, very small. Most of the members are older. We had some success with some of them. Because the programs were powerful and we didn't recognize that, they were misused by the political system. The political system began to take the youths and use them as role models and examples. The brothers were offered jobs at $100 or $200 a week and were given credit cards. They began to leave the community for places where they weren't effective. They were pulled into things that they weren't ready for; they got lost in these things. They had to come back home, in a sense.

The organization itself has had a lot of successes, as well as failures. SAND is moving into the services of youth employment, housing, and senior citizen escort.

The Twenties has established itself working with the community. They had a Community Day, and the very people that were complaining about the gangs at that particular time—they were trying to establish a youth day in this particular community. The Magnificent Twenties wanted to set up a booth, but the youth day committee did not want that; the committee thought the gang was too powerful. So rather than get into a fight, I had to sit down and explain to them about working with people who might not be what you're about, but you have to look at the positive things that they're doing. That community day was a positive effort. Even though the group did not want to work with them, the Twenties gave them $250 to start and the first donation they got for community day. The group really felt bad when they found that the money came from the very people they didn't want there. In fact, the only money they got was from the Magnificent Twenties. So youth day was set up. It had a lot to do with Kwansa, a cultural period from December 26 to January 5. In celebration, there were a lot of things that they did. They recognized the Puerto Rican sector of the community and began to celebrate Three Kings Day and that kind of thing. The

Twenties members volunteered to sit on some boards. They became more knowledgeable about the political system. They recognized what happened to them individually, as well as collectively.

We've also been working with tobacco growers, as we found fewer youth jobs coming from CETA. We recognized that the growers go south every year to employ 700 to 800 people, so we told them we have people right here in the city, willing to work tobacco and willing to get out there on the farm, because they need employment. We were trying to show them how we could save them money; they were trying to show us that the inner-city workers had come there before and torn up the tobacco. If we could control the youngsters there, however, they'd go along with the plan. Then we took certain members of the Magnificent Twenties and told them what we wanted. It worked. However, they had to deal with things like racism on the farm. The program worked from our end; it didn't work from the farmers' end. When the youngsters came out there, the farmers saw them as a threat. They thought they were coming to take over the farm. The youngsters were just coming out there to work for the summer, but farmers thought they were coming out there to take over completely.

There have been large successes with the particular gang that we've been counseling. We're continuing to work with insurance companies, putting together a job-readiness proposal. We're talking about 400 students going into the insurance companies. We are identifying young people who are going to work with other young people. All in all, real progress has been made.

Al Martin, Youth Identity Program, Inc.,
and Carl Hardrick, South Arsenal
Neighborhood Development Corporation (SAND)

Youth in Action

TOMMIE LEE JONES

With commentary by Patricia Fountain and Lewis Fields

TOMMIE LEE JONES: Chester, Pennsylvania, is a small city, 4.8 square miles, with a population about 50,000. When we began, the population was about 70,000. The white population began to move out, leaving it 80 percent black and 15 percent Hispanic. Youth in Action started from my working at a poverty program during the 1960s and 1970s. I worked as a field representative. I went from door to door to find out the problems in the homes, to see what we could do to help different families.

During this work, I found that the problem not being considered was our young people. Everyone decided that they would not involve our young people; they did not care about what was happening to young people in Chester. I decided to take on this problem myself and I began to work closely with the young people. About six months after I began to work, I was called into the office of the director. He asked what I intended, what I was trying to do. He said that his job depended upon whether I kept my nose out of other people's business. I asked him what he meant by that. He said his children were used to eating a certain way, used to dressing a certain way, and he was not going to let anyone stop this action. He thought the extra time I spent with the young people was a threat to his job; so I told him then that I would have to resign. I went to another job, working for the county welfare agency for children's youth services. As a nonprofessional, I was hired as an example of how nonprofessionals can work in a professional situation and do well. I found out that in this agency no one cared about giving services or meeting needs or finding problems or trying to help kids solve their problems. They were too busy trying to put kids in institutions. In a vicious circle, you put them in institutions, whereby you keep jobs going for probation officers; they saw me working people out of jobs. The heat became more intense. I had to resign from that job and started working for youths on my own.

I took my kids and opened my home to them. We would sometimes have 150 kids in my home, all over the house—downstairs, upstairs, in the cellar, anywhere we could find space. That's where we began to work. We got a grant from the Sun Oil Company, $15,000 for three years—$5,000 per year. Then we began to receive referrals from other agencies, children's youth services, family services, juvenile justice; we got walk-ins. The kids would come in and tell me they were having a lot of problems. Where can we get jobs? I'm having a baby, and I don't know what to do—my parents are busy having their own problems. They could not be bothered with kids. So what do you do when you have a one-parent family? You go to the streets and if there's nothing available for you to do, then you find a way to make a living. It could involve stealing cars, televisions, or tape recorders to sell. The kids began to confide in me. Remember, you have to be accepted in the community by youth in order for them to tell you their problems. If they don't trust you, they won't bother with you. I can assume that everyone here has gained—and worked hard to earn—that respect from the young people. The other thing is that you become suspect when you try to do something in your community, not only by the other agencies, but by the community people themselves. They want to know why you are interested in working with their young people. Are you getting rich? We had to raise our own funds. We sold chicken dinners; we had tag days, dances; we sold anything that we could get to sell, short of stealing. Different things were donated to us to sell. The first year we raised $1,200. That was a big plus for us, because we started out with $80—$80 I had to put up myself as seed money.

We had a large problem with drugs in our community. From age seven years up, either the youngsters were selling drugs or taking drugs. This was not my decision; the decision came from the youths themselves. I did not tell them what they needed. They told me what was needed from the community, what they needed to survive. They discussed all their problems; one was the need for a drug program. Immediately, we went out into the streets and started talking to some of the people involved in drug prevention and asked them if they would assist us in trying to start a drug program in Chester. This program eventually became so sophisticated that other people in the political structure came in, after we had done all the groundwork, after I had taken drug addicts into my home and tried to detoxify them. (I tried this cold turkey, but I found they were only leading me on, after two, three weeks of lying around.) At last we got the drug program off the ground; it is now known as the Delaware County Comprehensive Drug Program, not Youth in Action. Our name was never mentioned, nor the fact that we initiated the whole process.

We were incorporated in 1971, and we became quite sophisticated in our peer-counseling concept. If a young person has a problem, who is better to help him than another young person who has experienced that problem? That's how our agency works, on a peer-counseling concept. We have a youth council that's very good. The members meet every Sunday at 3:00 P.M. at my home, and I cook a meal for them. That shows that they're appreciated and that they're wanted there. It provides a relaxed atmosphere. From relaxing, the truth comes to light. The kids will tell you all their problems, what they would like to see done, and how to do it. Kids themselves know exactly what their problems are, and they know how to combat them. But adults do not seem to want to listen. Children should be seen and not heard; that was said in the days when things weren't as complicated as they are now. Young people do have a lot to say. If we would only stop and listen to them, some of our problems could be solved. We get a lot of resistance from the city itself because, as one police officer said, What are we trying to do, get a lot of them laid off? They live by the problems in our city, with our young people. Chester has a population of 50,000. Out of that 50,000, 19,000 are young—between the ages of six and eighteen. We have a lot of young people, mostly females, and our young ladies do cause a lot of the problems, but I had never before thought about using them to stop the problems. We can use that as one of our basic techniques in trying to solve any problem.

We didn't really have a gang problem at first, but Philadelphia had a bad gang problem, and we sit between Philadelphia and Delaware. Everything that's bad flows over into Chester. One day one of the young men told me that a gang war was starting. Unfortunately, before we could get involved, two young men did lose their lives. We were brought in later when one of the young people asked what we could do to stop this. We said we'd see how much courage they had. We arranged a boxing match in the inner city and invited everyone. We started around 9:00 A.M., and they fought up until about 9:00 P.M. Well, everybody was very tired, but we've never had another gang problem there.

We don't have a gang problem in Chester now, but we do have other problems. We have a 47 percent unemployment rate. About 200 of our businesses and industries have left Chester. Most of our families have one parent, mostly mothers. There is no male figure in the home. We do have men, but they're just not visible. The ratio is twenty to one. We act as an advocate for the youth in the schools. In our school district, we have only one high school, with 3,500 young people. When any student has a problem, he doesn't go to children youth services or family services or his parents; he comes to Youth in Action because he knows that we try to do our best without condemning anyone from the beginning.

One of the problems has been that we don't give our young people a chance—we condemn them. I can feel a quiet surge happening over our country with our young people. They are ready to strike out against us adults, because we have not shown them any leadership about which way to go.

We share the same experience of many groups in not having ample funds. The largest grant that we have ever had was $35,000. I thought that was maybe God-sent. We've been working now without funds for two years, and I don't know how much longer we'll be able to continue. Our staff members are being paid through CETA (the Comprehensive Employment and Training Act). I've been volunteering, since the conception of the program. I'm not eligible for funding, because my husband has a job. My husband is known as Big Jim. Sometimes the kids call him John Wayne. When there is a problem of fighting, all he has to do is walk up and quietly say, "Break it up," and that's what happens. He's six feet four. He's also very active—my whole family is active—in the program. I have five children and three grandsons, and everybody plays a part in Youth in Action. We call it Youth in Action because the youths are active in our programs. We try to get them involved in every aspect of living, especially the political part. That has a lot to do with whether we live or die. The more input they have in the structure, the better the chance of making some changes. We have to teach our young people from the beginning how to live in society.

PATRICIA FOUNTAIN: I'm a job career developer and counselor at Youth in Action. It is my job to try to find some jobs for those persons who don't have jobs. I work especially with people from the ages of fourteen to twenty-one, sometimes older. When they come to talk to me, the first thing I try to find out is what kind of things they have done, what kind of jobs, what they would like to do. After we go through that process, I am able many times to find them jobs in areas they would like and would be able to do. You shouldn't give a person a job if he or she wouldn't be there any longer than a day or a week, just to say that you got them a job. I try to find something that they could do for quite a while, that they would be happy with. Sometimes I have to set up interviews for them. I have to call them constantly about the time. Sometimes I have to take them to their interviews. If I stay with them, they will be there until the interview.

I also coordinate job seminars. For the last two weeks, we've been trying to get the youngsters exposed to the different jobs that are available. I work with the students in the high school; I want them to know what's out there, how they can become more marketable, the kinds of skills they need for some of the jobs. We go to job seminars. We visit colleges. When I was in college, I was a financial aid officer. I let the youngsters know about the kinds of money available for college—basic opportunity grants, foundation money, church funds, different things. We visit companies. I try to get around to all the companies in our area, learn the kinds of people that they are looking for. We try to have a working relationship so that if the firms need a person with a particular skill, I can say that I have somebody qualified for that job. I try to work on their positive attitude, positive thought. Our organization is a kind of whole-pie organization; we work with the whole person. We work with his or her physical self; we work with the intellectual self. We work with the emotional stability of the person, to prepare them, so they see that they can do things. We work on the spiritual side. Between January 1978 and 1980, we were able to place ninety-six youths in permanent jobs. With a 47 percent unemployment rate in the city of Chester, somehow we've managed to wave our magic wands. I got to know some of the business people in the city; we played on their sympathy and asked them for jobs. You have to do a lot of politicking and a lot of crying and praying to keep a nonprofit community-based organization going.

LEWIS FIELDS: Let me give you some examples of the problems we encounter. In dealing with jobs like the CETA program, with Delaware County and Philadelphia, there are only so many slots allocated to the city of Chester. Three or four years ago, our kids had to go through two interviews for these jobs. For one of them, they had to go to the manpower office, located about fifteen miles out of the city in another area. Contact was not always made with the young people when they received a call from manpower. It's often hard to get a young person at home; he might not have a telephone, nobody picks up the phone, or a kid doesn't get a message. In this case, usually manpower did not attempt the second contact; the next applicant was rewarded. Accordingly, three years ago, we were only getting 150 jobs of 250 slots available to the city. The kids from the suburbs, not the city, would receive those jobs because they were closer to the office for the second interview. In addition, we get no money for mileage, taking kids back and forth for interviews. Any time that we have to take a group of kids to an interview fifteen miles away—we have to do that four times a week in March, April, and May—it's hard on our pockets. But, in doing that, we have improved our score, so that every year, of 500 or 600 slots allocated to the city or county, Youth in Action has provided assistance, not only for work at our site but around the city, for 350 youths each summer. We're still helping 250 youths with applications.

We go further with job development. When a person came to the city to build churches, for instance, I sought out this person. I told him he would need some young people. He said to get a group of 50 young kids within two weeks. We had 125 young kids all lined up on the doorsteps to get the jobs. When he interviewed them, he hired 125 on the spot.

We talk about youths filling jobs in the private sector; we go to gas stations, small businesses, newspapers, small stores—any place to try to find jobs. Our youth do after-school tutoring, recreational aid, and some clerical work. They also get into cultural activities.

Our young people help each other, with peer counseling. Our college students who have grown up in our program come back during the summer; they teach our high school students some of the things that they need to know as far as life skills are concerned. Our youth counselors are 25 to 65 young people; our counseling is based on the problems that we have in Chester. We know education is a problem. We know sports and recreation are dull in Chester. We know that employment is a problem. We know that young people need to get into the civic, political arena to learn about how a city can grow. Fifteen of our youth council visited Washington, D.C., for the Youth Alliance Seminar last year. They met a lot of other youth in Washington, so that it was very exciting for them to come back and share their experience with their own youth council.

We do not have good recreation facilities in the whole city of Chester. We have two gyms—the YMCA on the west side and the YMCA on the central side. The gyms are inadequate. They don't have the things that other gyms have in the suburbs. Five miles from the city limits, you would see them have nice clubs, nice courts, nice nets, all the things we need in the city. We can just go and look at those; we cannot participate outside our city. We also have drug counseling. We have people come from Crozier Medical Hospital and other drug prevention programs to talk to some of the drug addicts and to try to encourage them in helping themselves, helping their neighbors, and helping the children in their neighborhood. We have a day care service. The parents have to work and have to leave these kids at home. We charge no fee for the kids to stay there. We use the city's free lunch program. We protect the children on the playgrounds. We have vans now. We transport our kids, not too far but reasonable distances to get them involved with other environments and other communities. We took fifteen young ladies to a male institution detention center outside Chester, in Delaware County, for the annual social night.

We have cultural activities, including ones at Christmas. We talk about the three kings and we talk about the black Christmas; in the eyes of little kids who are not familiar with the different holidays, they always ask why Santa Claus doesn't look like them. We make our own Santa Claus. At our Christmas party, there is no fee; the toys are donated (we had to search for them) by churches, army barracks, and small businesses that had toys that needed to be fixed. Our workers fixed the toys. We got a tree. We made it a wholesome type of Christmas for those kids who did not have Christmas. After the Christmas party, we had cake and juice and ice cream, with an extra fifty youngsters. They didn't want any toys, but they wanted to participate with the ice cream and cake. Some of the other cultural activities we try to have are on-the-spot activities. Our talent show, for instance, had singers, bands, comedians, all given the chance to perform on stage. This talent show was set up by the youths themselves. We profit because the kids say to themselves that they can sing, they can do it, they had a chance, and they must go on from there.

We have all types of activities. As part of a continuing educational program, we go to universities to look at the college atmosphere, to see how youths get into a university, how to get into a state school, to take the youths out of their environment. They always see universities and such on television or in magazines or in catalogs; they never visit these institutions. At the colleges, some of our young people get a chance to mingle with the college students and to sample that terrible college food. It's not like Mom's cooking at home. This is another part of our continuing education program.

In setting up a visit to a college, we make sure that we have a workshop or conference with the college staff—the financial aid people, people with applications; they go step-by-step to explain the different procedures on how to get into a college for that next semester or, for those in the eleventh grade, what they need to do to prepare for that particular college. If they're not up to the academic standards of that particular university, they are put in a clerical, technical skills program, or in a summer program so that they can get into the particular college or institution. We took twenty-five trips between 1979 and 1980, with 540 kids participating. The students need to know the rules and regulations. We make contact with the parents, too. We have to make sure what college the kids want to attend. We do research on what type of school is appropriate—a two-year school, state school, or university—depending on the academic background of the individual.

Another part of our program involves sports and recreation. We need recreation twenty-four hours a day as far as our young people are concerned, because we need something to occupy their minds. During the summer, recreation is a necessity. We keep the young people out of trouble, keep them from mingling with the wrong people, who would lead them into difficult times on the street. Mr. Jones is the nucleus of our basketball program. For our junior program, ages thirteen to fifteen, he's had at least nine city junior championships in fifteen years. We have eight teams during the winter in the Chester city recreational basketball league. Our league didn't have uniforms. Having been in the world of basketball, I know that a complete uniform motivates kids. We now have three teams of fifteen—forty-five uniforms. The kids do not take their uniforms home; they give them to me. I go to Mrs. Jones's house (her electric bill is $100 a month, by the time the season's over). We wash them, we dry them, we take care of them, and we bring them to the games. We've been doing this for about four years. In doing that, we stimulated the community. The other teams were in the same situation, with no uniforms. When we had a complete uniform, they said the league looks much better. Then we helped them get sponsors so that the whole league would be uniformed. Both of the teams are now fully dressed, and they really motivated the whole league as far as the young people in Chester are concerned.

We had one fellow who used to fight everybody in the project. We transferred his temper into coaching. He was a loser, but he felt if he joined our organization, maybe he'd be a winner. This year, this young man took a Cinderella team, which he coached last year, from 0 and 14 to 14 and 2 this year. This is what a person can do if you give him a chance.

Our funding is to establish basketball programs, because it takes too much to finance a football team. We have a senior basketball project also, created four years ago.

I always wanted to go to the NBA (National Basketball Association), and I'm just like everybody else. When we would play at the playground, we'd say we want to go to the NBA. The only reason I want to go to the NBA is that I want the cars. I want to buy my mother a house and my sister a house. I know I can do this if I get in the NBA. You have more and more people coming out of college into professional sports, but there's a limit to how many people can make it. Because we have only one high school in Chester, you have only twelve individuals who can make that high school team, out of 3,500 students. They say to themselves they want to play, they've got a good game. They figure they can go to college to play basketball.

I did a year and a half of research; I wrote to the NCAA (the National Collegiate Athletics Association). I wrote to the different college and the athletic directors of universities and two-year schools. I told them we had a smaller program which we would like to extend to give a second chance to our young people—eighteen to twenty-one—to go to college. My first year, in 1976, they gave me ten games, but we had to be self-funded, self-sponsored, raise our own money for our uniforms. We played against universities and state college freshman teams, before the varsity, at their home courts, on major basketball floors. This gave our youths more incentive. I found out that this had never been done in the nation on this level. We practice one time on Sunday for about four hours. I loosen my tie, and I holler real loud. There are certain fundamentals they need to know under pressure. This is the first time that these young people really have a crowd. Half of these young people or 75 percent of them did not play high school ball, so they're on the college floor for the first time, playing the crowd for the first time. This motivates them to continue their education or to find a good job. Our young ladies said we had to have some cheerleaders. Cheerleaders make you win, and, believe me, they made us win this year and last year, too. We didn't have a cheerleader coach, so we have one person on each of the groups be the captain if everybody wants her to be. They practice after school two times a week and they do a remarkable job. We have a couple of young men who are receiving their college educations playing basketball. I don't know what we would do without our volunteers. We cannot get out and work with the kids individually, so our volunteer coaches go to the games and talk to our players after the game and give them counseling throughout the week on mistakes they made.

We had a senior citizens day; the senior citizens bring their grandchildren in and they talk to Mrs. Jones about some of their problems with their grandchildren and the community. When we're having our annual banquet, we bring in professionals and government representatives to address our young people on the problems of the day. Kids recognize their parents on these occasions. At the Youth in Action tenth annual anniversary banquet, one woman was given a money tree from her kids. This is what we need in the community— a return to the family and helping each other. Mrs. Jones is dealing with a civic matter, bringing the blue route to Chester, a four-lane highway connecting to another highway on the waterfront. This will bring in many businesses in five or ten years, with 50,000 jobs for the entire community.

*Carl Hardrick, South Arsenal
Neighborhood Development
Corporation (SAND)*

*Tommie Lee Jones,
Youth in Action*

Part
Two

Discussion on the Youths' Experiences
and on
Youth Crime and Public Policy

Peter Berger,
Boston College

Left to right:
Robert Selby, House of Umoja
Lewis Fields, Youth in Action
Irma Torres Colon, Dispensario
  San Antonio, Inc.

Discussion

The Youth's Experiences

Robert (Fat Rob) Allen, the House of Umoja: Let me start by telling how I got in contact with the House of Umoja, how I got involved with the program, what I'm into now, and what my job function is. I was a gang leader for ten years. In 1972, Sister Fattah had a conference for all the gangs in Philadelphia. Before that I had been to so many meetings, and people had made so many promises that it was a regular thing to me. The first thing I thought was: well, are these people the same, what are they trying to do? A brother in the House invited me to the gang conference. When I went, I met Sister Fattah and her husband, Dave. I heard them speak about a human life, and that's what made me take a liking to Sister Fattah. At that time, I didn't know what a human life meant. To take a human life—to me, it didn't mean any thing then. She made me aware. Her husband, Dave, was talking about us killing each other out in the street; every time the cops ride up in their blue-and-white car, we take our guns and we throw them under the car. But as soon as another brother comes, we're going to blow his brains out.

I took a liking to Sister Fattah.

After the conference, I started working in the community with other organizations. But I found that other organizations are governed by the administration of the city; you can do but so many things. I couldn't deal with that kind of organization, where I can't speak out or say what I feel about my people and what should be done. I have to work where I can move around and talk about different issues. After I heard the sister talking, I started getting involved in community work, because I was a gang leader and almost everybody listened to me. When I went to the House of Umoja, my first job was working with the brothers in prisons. My job was to write them, correspond with them, help them to get out, and help them to get settled in society. Today, I heard a lot of different things from different parts of the country; and to me we all have the same problem—we've all been bitten by the same dog. We all identify ourselves differently, but we all have the same problem.

At the House of Umoja, I started working with the gangs. I started setting up gang councils, for something like twenty gangs. With a gang problem, we bring two brothers from each gang and we'll sit at the table and we iron things out before they get serious. In 1969, 1970, and 1972, there were forty to forty-five killings every year. After Sister Fattah had the gang conference, things started dying down. The House of Umoja wasn't given the credit due it. That was given to the city administration. When people come to the city to find out how to deal with their problems, the city tells them to talk with city-funded agencies. The city doesn't send them to us.

Because I was a great factor of the problem, I couldn't ease away from the problem. Sister Fattah and many other community leaders made me aware that I was a leader in a negative way and I could be a leader in a positive way. I heard different people today say what a gang is, but I want to tell you what a gang is. A gang is what you make it. A gang is the people who hang out; they don't have to be negative or positive. It's what you make them. The House of Umoja was unique; no one there ever promised us nothing and it was so different for me not to hear anybody promise you something. Some programs give you a couple of summer jobs and cool you off for the summer, but how about the other ten months, when they close down the playground? When they close down the recreation centers?

A gang is the most positive thing we have for black people anywhere in the world; when one person does something, they all do it. The only problem is that when we continue to commit bodily harm against each other; then you have a problem. But if we do it in a positive way, there's no other organization, no religious group, that's more together than a gang. When some people think of a gang, they think of violence. I don't. I've been to prison, I've been shot eight times in six months. But because of people like Sister Fattah, I can't go back and do negative things. If I do negative things, since people see me working in the community with Sister Fattah so much, that would affect the organization. One thing I learned from her was patience and how to deal with people. I used to flare up at meetings and tell the people I don't want to hear it—I sit down now and listen.

No matter what kind of a program we set up, we always put the brothers in it, the brothers who pledge not to gang-war anymore. In 1974, we had no gang wars, and, in 1975, we kept more brothers alive. We need programs like the House of Umoja. Too many people just want to take young people that are now hard-core gang members and lock them up in jail with adults. That's not right. With more places like the House of Umoja, we can do more for our young people. At the House of Umoja sometimes we go six or seven months without any money; money doesn't mean anything to us. This is a job that has to be done beyond nine to five. At the House of Umoja we only work twenty-four hours a day, any time of day. The people that you pay $40,000 or $50,000 a year to deal with these problems can't even deal with them. When there is a problem in the street, those people call us. Why are they getting the money, not us? Our program has got to be a success, because the kids are successes. They're not going to jail, they're going back to school. They're getting themselves in order. Nobody can come to our community if we don't want him there. When there's a bad gang problem, nobody can go to the store, nothing moves.

But the city administration wanted to solve this gang problem itself. After we settled the gang problems, the city made employment bad for us. If you can't get a job, you have to sell drugs, you have to stick something up, you have to do whatever you can to survive. That's what it's about—survival. People always talk about the violent things we do, but they never talk about the positive things we do. The only time that you get something in the paper is when you kill somebody. If you do something positive, you have to go 100 pages to find it. Sister Fattah took on all the gangs in the city. If something exploded, it would have been terrible. It didn't; everybody gave her respect, and we have respect. We all sit at the table, and we make decisions collectively—we don't just go out and do things. We make each other aware of what we are doing. Any problem that comes up in the black community—we deal with it. It doesn't have to be a gang problem; it can be any kind of problem. If you tell gangs to stop what they're doing because it's wrong, you have to have an alternative for them. Don't make them stop what they're doing if there is nothing else for them to do; then they have to go back to their old ways. The House of Umoja has been in existence for twelve years. It started without any money; that should show people that it must have known what it was doing.

Tommie Lee Jones said that people in your own community and your neighborhood can give you problems. That's from jealousy; jealousy is from a lack of confidence in yourself. You see somebody else doing something. You don't have enough confidence in yourself to do it, so you want to bring that person down. I can't understand how all the black people are made to pull all the black people down. That's definitely wrong. Even in the year I stayed in prison, a jail cell was better than some homes.

People say the brothers used to stop gang war at eighteen. I didn't stop until I was about twenty-three; that's a five-year difference. There's a lack of communication. I'm not going to let the young people get so far away that we can't sit down and talk to them. You hear a lot of young people saying, "I want to be like him." But I say, "Be like I am now, not like I was." If it wasn't for Sister Fattah and her husband, Dave, I probably would be dead in jail for killing somebody; that's how bad things were. We don't get along well with the police department, because the police don't communicate with us. When you do get a police officer in the community to understand the problem, he's gone, he's sent on traffic duty somewhere. The authorities have to get him out of there; they send in a bunch of rookies. First thing, they want to pull out their guns and their sticks and beat you on the head. When we went to New York City in 1976 for the gang conferences there, you know, it kind of took me out. The police department was taking us around,[1] giving us dinner. If the police had done this in Philly, I wouldn't have gone. The police used to take us for rides; they would take us into other neighborhoods and make us walk by fifty dudes from opposing gangs.

The brothers in jail are like most brothers. We all grew up together; we all knew each other. When we were incarcerated, we all got along. When we come out on the street, why can't we get along? When I came out, I came out thinking that way. I took the college courses in jail. I didn't let that year go by and let it be wasted; I used it. In my résumé, you know I've been to prison. But I've had four years of college, because Sister Fattah inspired me. My main concern is finding employment for young people and keeping them on the job. We tell all the gang members from all over the city if they do wrong, we have to deal with that. We're not going to let the city tear down what Sister Fattah did for us. One thing about Sister, she never tries to take all the credit; if the young people didn't want to stop gang wars, then they wouldn't stop. But we need her advice and guidance.

We don't want anybody to give us anything or do anything for us, but we want help to do things ourselves. If you look around your city, you have maybe ten thousand houses that are old and run-down. This can create jobs for us, to go in there and fix things, because we have these skills. About basketball, you have to remember one thing: don't let your young people think that they can play basketball and make a living. Let them get an education along with that; in case the contract doesn't come through, they have something else to fall back on. We have a lot of people with talent who lie on the corner and drink wine. What the brothers and sisters are doing in Chester is good, because they make the kids go to school, get an education. We do have some people who make it in basketball. That's good. But I know people who got

---

[1] In 1976 Robert Woodson, who was then the director of criminal justice programs for the National Urban League, convened a conference that brought together ex-gang members and representatives of the National Black Police Association. They exchanged experiences and opinions on common concerns. The black police group hosted the youngsters at a Harlem restaurant.

away from education, who think school is a joke. The teachers don't care if they learn. We have to start our own schools and teach our own people what we want them to know.

I'm grateful to Sister Fattah and I'm thankful to God that He sent her to help us. I always have respect for black women. They are strong; they keep us on our feet. Behind every successful man is a woman. Sister is a beautiful person. Her helping me has inspired me. This conference has inspired me to do even more, because I know you all have similar problems.

We started doing plays. We gave a play in honor of Sister Fattah. In the beginning of the play, we took all our guns and threw them into a trash can, showing people that we have given the credit to her, not the city. The mayor was talking about turning in guns. I turned in a broken gun and got some real guns. We were not going to give the mayor our weapons.

We should put our ideas together and try to do things. We ought to take different ideas back to our cities. Gangs have grown members, too. As the brother said, I'm going to be for the Empire until I die. I'm going to be a gang member, but I'm going to be one in a positive way. I'm going to try to make all the brothers see that we need to be positive. If all people are like that, we can do something. When the authorities stopped the gangs, they broke up the togetherness. Every time I went out there and busted somebody in the head or shot somebody, these people got money for programs. They started picking the leaders from the crowd and giving us a job. When our boys were stranded, because we had jobs, we kept them cool. We started coming to the program people and said, "Look, I got a job. Here are my ten homies [friends]; get them jobs." Then we started running into problems. When I was with other organizations, they were telling me I couldn't hang out with the brothers, because I was part of them and I wear suits and stuff. But that's not where it's at. You have to go in the street and get ideas from people, find out what they want to do.

At the House of Umoja, every year we put out a survey. We find out what the people want—how they like our help. We always get 100 percent positive replies. We're trying to rebuild houses on a whole block now; that's the sister's dream, to create an urban boy's town. Anything I can do to help, I'm going to do. We need more people to work along with us; we get phone calls from all over to help. Gang members are working with so many different people. We've got ex-gang members who are committeemen; they're senators, they're congressmen. It's not that we don't have any sense. Anybody can learn. If a teacher doesn't want to teach me, I'm going to learn anyway. If she teaches it, I'm going to learn it. I graduated from college. I gang-warred, but I waited until after class, because I had a lot of responsibility. I was responsible for people's lives. If I killed somebody, then there would be a big write-up in the paper: "Ex-gang member working for Sister Fattah kills somebody." She doesn't need any negative things like that. We should all think positive.

I want to hear from the younger people, what they think of these ideas. Maybe we can get some ideas from them and from the older people, put them together, and bring something positive from this conference. One day we could have a national gang conference, where a whole national sample of gangs could meet. We're teaching our young people how to register and how to vote. When you vote, you have a voice. We're getting our own people in office. One day I plan to run for political office myself.

ROBERT SELBY, the House of Umoja: I came to the House of Umoja four years ago. I used to live in South Philly. I had bad family problems. I had been in an institution. My father put me away, because I was hanging out with a gang. I had a choice. I went there and I liked it. I started seeing it was about being positive. Where I come from, there were a lot of negative things—people stealing, gang-warring, shooting, and all that. School was a drag. I didn't like school. People talked about school, whether I wanted to go back to school. I was skeptical. I didn't want to go, but one of the brothers at the house sat down with me. I stayed there the whole summer and went back to school in September.

GEORGE AMOS, SAND: I'm trying to do right and to help people on my own level. I talk to them, tell them that isn't any way to be. I see some little kid throwing bottles, and I try to talk to him. If I can't talk to him, I send him to Carl Hardrick, to see if Carl could talk to him.

I also help Carl with applications for the people who need summer jobs. I help them fill out their applications properly. If they make a mistake, I call them in and tell them they've got to fix it. When you take the application to CRT, if anything is wrong with it, CRT doesn't want it. People do not give you the job; they just set your paper aside and look at another application.

We also work with young people, with different people who come from New York, Boston, all over. They come to Hartford, and they have African dances, with all sorts of African traditions. We take care of security and keep everything friendly. After that, they have a dinner and sit down to a conference. Everybody talks. Then the people go back home and do the same kind of thing with their own people in New York or wherever they come from.

CARL HARDRICK, SAND: In terms of the kinds of things that George Amos is doing, what's important is the influence he has on people younger than he is, people that I could not talk to. If I'm able to talk to someone from fourteen to eighteen, I can't reach someone maybe twelve or eight or nine going in that same direction. He's able to do that, because they look up to him. That's why we have to put out those positive directions.

The level of thinking starts early in a negative direction. You have to use those brothers in a positive way to curb that negative thinking. It's important that you give them good examples. If they believe in them, they will do the same.

ALBERT (CRAZY CAT) MEJIAS, ICRY: I'm on the Roundtable board of ICRY, and I'm the president of the Manhattan chapter of the Savage Riders. I've been in ICRY for almost five years. I was one of the first with ICRY, also with the Ching-A-Lings and the Savage Goal. I've been involved in training, unemployment, housing rehabilitation, and legal services. I've always worked as a volunteer in crisis intervention. I was one of the first security officers at the Beacon Theater and other places.

DARRYL (TEE) RODGERS, SEY YES: I'm originally from the South Side of Chicago. I moved to Los Angeles in 1969 and from 1969 until 1970, I had an open letter from the Blackstone Rangers in Chicago that authorized me to start my own chapter of the Blackstone Rangers in Los Angeles. At one time the membership numbered in the thousands. At that particular time, they were no longer called the Blackstone Rangers; they were the Almighty Black Peace-Stone Nation. Unfortunately, you do not know the history of Los Angeles. Los Angeles is the land of liquid sunshine and golden opportunity. You can come there and be anything that you want—anything; nobody cares.

V.G. and I have been in situations where the Los Angeles Police Department has surrounded us, and we had the helicopter above. There's a gang on this side and a gang on that side, and a ping pong table. We sat down at the table and negotiated peace treaties right then and there. We have a four-year peace treaty with another club called the Avenues; it's one of the only treaties in Los Angeles that still stands to this day. I gave V.G. exactly six hours to get a treaty between the Blackstones and the Avenues, or we were going to just kill them off; it didn't make any difference to us. The only thing that separated us was the double yellow line down the middle of the street. V.G. persuaded me to stop using my gang influence in a negative way, but use it to establish peace. I joined the staff at SEY YES.

The director of SEY YES is getting old now; he failed to mention some things about our program. I guess that's why V.G. brought me with him. He forgot to mention the rap sessions that we have, maybe because a lot of times we don't invite him. Our program is geared like almost every program here to the streets, with people who are of the streets. That's what makes it work.

We have an athletic program to deal with kids in elementary school. Our philosophy and ideology go a little bit deeper than the correctional institutions and the schools. If we can get to a youngster at the time when he starts thinking, "I want to be like so and so," we can direct him.

Again I agree with Fat Rob (Robert Allen); I am not only of city power, but I am of a world power. I have been chosen and selected to say, "We can go this way or we can go that way." I've been chosen to hold, directly and indirectly, in my hands, the matter of life and death. If I can get to somebody between the ages of six and eight years old and tell him that I have been into this thing and I know what it's all about, I can show him it's not cool. I say, "Hey, I've been there, the whole shot, juvenile justice system and everything, and it's just not cool." They say, "Hey, we go to the movies—and they've got *The Godfather*. Everybody thinks that's cool. But the reality is not like that at all.

At that time, we ask them, "What do you want to do? How do you want to work this? How are you going to run this?" The basketball programs, the football programs, at that time in life, are essential. The kids don't want to go to school, because school isn't cool. But we'll play a little sports and see what happens.

The other thing that we've got like your programs is a neighborhood watch. We are not sophisticated with the cars and radios and everything, but we have what is called a grapevine in Los Angeles. The grapevine is strong. To give you a prime example, we just got a call here in Washington that two people from a rival gang have been killed. I don't care where I go, what I'm doing, or who I'm with, I'm going to find out what's what in the neighborhood.

The other thing that V. G. did not mention is our work in area five in Los Angeles, with the school district. In Los Angeles, gangs are so spread out that the only place that you can meet—and where most of the problems happen—is on school grounds. I found out that if I wanted anything in the world, I should not stay home but go to school. If I wanted drugs, I went to school. If I wanted a new watch, I went to school. If I wanted a new tape for my car, I went to school—and got it from the teachers.

This is where crisis intervention comes in, because everybody is there at that particular time. We have a thing called opportunity transfer, where one kid is sent from one school to another school. If he's in one area of L.A. and he's transferred to another, then he has to go back to his neighborhood. If there is a fight there, when he comes back to school, kids are going to jam him at school; they're going to jump on him. This is where crisis intervention comes in; we stop the violence right there.

We do in-service training for gang leaders, for all the school administrators, for psychiatrists, for almost anybody in Los Angeles interested in gang behavior or the structure of gangs. I give workshops, or rap sessions, to brothers in gangs who are looking for alternatives, another way of life.

In SEY YES, we have ten males and females who have graduated from college. Some of them are pursuing careers in law. One of my brothers is studying law. Unfortunately, in his early life, he did two and a half years at Cook County jail on three counts of murder; he was acquitted later. Now he is studying to become a lawyer.

The program has a dramatic impact on each individual. Our program is set up to help each individual. We cannot set up criteria to say, "This will work for this person, and this will work for that person." That is why I like the program. I've been like Rob. I've been hooked up with other programs that tell us you've got to put your suit on and you can't hang out with the gangs anymore. I wouldn't be here if I hadn't been there first.

The program that V.G. sets up is like the confrontation between us when he and I first met at an elementary school. Being one of the leaders of the blacks at that particular time, I had to gather money for the nation. There was a community-based meeting where people discuss CETA jobs, and the whole shot; I was there bidding for my park. I had no prior knowledge that V.G. was in the audience. After I got through speaking, I came into contact with the notorious V.G. Angels. In two hours, I was introduced to V.G.

I told V.G. I'm eight thousand strong. My neighborhood is larger than your city. Why am I going to give up all this to come work for you or listen to you when I call my own shots? I can go onto any campus in Los Angeles. In between passing bells at school—in five minutes— in a bathroom I can find out who went to jail, who didn't go to jail, who got shot and is going to get shot, whose mama put him out, whose mama is mad at him, whose mama is having an affair—and collect all the dues. Why am I going to give all this up to work with you? [Laughter.]

V.G. just said, "As much as you run your mouth, let me put you in public relations." I started as a public relations officer, and I worked my way up from that.

What is unique about our program is the way it's set up to help the individual. For my problem, I said, "If I'm going to work for you, you've got to make me work." He said, "Oh no, if you want to work, you work on your own. I'm not going to make you do anything."

So that was our relationship. Brothers on the street and of the street know who is cool and who is not cool, who they can talk to, who they can trust and who they can't. This is an unwritten law, it's universal.

IRMA TORRES COLON, Dispensario San Antonio: I want to talk about my experience in life, and La Playa de Ponce is part of it. I started with a group of girls. We work in the community, helping a lot of girls with problems.

I was living with my father and stepmother in La Playa de Ponce; I had problems with my stepmother. All my life, I lived with my step-mother and my father. Then I meet a friend named Wanda. She told me, "Irma, I want to take you to a group of girls." One morning, I did go to the center and met the people there. They asked me about myself, my age, whether I was in school. I didn't like school; I wasn't studying because of problems at home, with my father and my stepmother.

I joined the group. The people at the center show us a lot of things: how to cook, how to sew, how to care for babies. We work, we make men's wallets. I like sports. I play basketball and volleyball. In Puerto Rico, the girls play basketball well. We are stronger than the boys. I'm strong, because I work hard. I like to work hard.

The group also has a teacher who shows us how to cook. I'm a housewife, because I know all about the things in my house. I do all the things. I cook, I iron, I help my stepmother cook. I help my cousin, too. I want to work, and the group helped me get work.

I started working with a pre-job program for boys and girls at school. The people at the program told us we had to study. So I started studying. I took the tests for high school and I passed. I'm working with the program, with a lot of girls and boys. I work repairing houses. We work with the community; the community helps us, too.

All this has happened because of Sister Isolina Ferré. She loves all the young boys and girls, and she helps us. I want to give thanks to Sister Isolina Ferré, because she helped me a lot.

And my friend asked me, "Irma, are you going to Washington?" "Yes, I'm going to Washington." He said, "Well, good luck; you're going to have good luck." I have this privilege in my life, and I want all my friends to think about that because I want them to visit one day. I'm nervous. [Laughter.] When I was living with my father and my stepmother, I didn't have this opportunity to come to Washington.

I like to play sports and help the other boys and girls. Sister Isolina has helped the community, and the girls and the boys on drugs. She helped a lot there because there are no more drugs. We play a lot of sports. The girls work hard, more than the boys. We have six groups that work in different places in the community. The girls tell me I work like a maniac. I like to work hard. I'm going to show you some pictures. You can pass them. This is the work the girls and boys do, in La Playa de Ponce, and I want to give the same because I have experience, and give the thanks to Sister Isolina because she's an angel. I love the Sister, and thank you.

JERRY WRIGHT, Youth Identity Program: First, I want to tell you a little bit about my life history. I grew up in Harlem, where you might see your dinner walking across the floor, with a rat. I lost two brothers and a sister in fires. That's just how it was, you know.

I went through a lot of changes. I went to school. I was doing all right in school until a certain time. When my mother and father separated, I didn't know what to do. I didn't know who to turn to. I couldn't go to my mother and ask her the things that I would ask my father, so I just turned to the street.

I joined the Black Spades. There was a lot of unity in it; it was like a family. We started doing a lot of crazy things. I stuck up people, broke into stores—different things. I went to jail; I did time. I met someone who's my supervisor now, and he told me about the program. I went to the program. I didn't know what to expect. I didn't think it could help me, because I was satisfied with what I was doing, because I took what I needed.

I met Al Martin, and we considered him Papa Spade because he helped us a lot. He showed us the way.

Right now, I'm working at Rikers Island[2] everyday, trying to help the younger people. We go to court and represent them, try to get their charges lowered, get them to come to the program if we can. We work with the Housing Authority police. We give a lot of presentations at different schools.

As far as Rikers Island is concerned, a lot of people don't understand what is going on there. We have a lot of friction with the Corrections Department, because we get to see exactly what goes on within an institution. It's rough in there; only the strong survive in an institution. Some kid on the street might have just been hanging out with the wrong crowd, going to a party. Someone gives him a pistol. He gets busted. What's a pistol? He never even shot the pistol. Before you know, he's in jail. He's in there, and somebody walks up to him and

[2] Rikers Island is a pretrial detention center in New York City. Many juveniles are sent there to await either trial or processing for placement within the state prison system.

83

uses a certain term, like "bust this around your sneakers" and, "I want to take your hoods." In other words, they want to rape him. He's not a fighter, so he is raped. It's rough in there.

We work with the youths who have real problems. Sometimes it's their home life, or they might be hanging out with the wrong crowd. We need to show them the right way. The older people already know what's going on, because they've been there. They have their own problems; they have to struggle to survive. A lot of times they have big bills. They have to deal with this and deal with that. They can't even make a meeting at school. You come home with a note saying that your parent has to be at school. Your mother is telling you, "I'm too busy." Your father is not there; he can't go. You go back to school. Everyone else's parents might be there, but not yours. This affects you. You want to turn away from school. You don't want to deal with it. You're on the street. There are drugs out there, and a lot of different things going on.

I go home sometimes, after work. A lot of fellows I used to be with are out on corners selling drugs. I try to talk to them and tell them what's happening with the programs out there, what's available to them, what they can do to help themselves.

It's hard. I'm going to school. I work. I've got two kids of my own to think about. The program has helped me. Without it, I would probably have been back in jail. I wouldn't be here now, talking to you.

When I joined the Black Spades, it was something new to me—it was an adventure, something I never did before. I wanted to get out there and see what life is all about, like anybody else does. That was what was there, because the neighborhoods were rough. Either you joined a gang, or you were a punk, an outsider. Instead of playing basketball or baseball, I was robbing people. I guess that came from a broken home, not having a father, losing brothers and sisters in fires.

The program benefits me; it shows me where I'm headed. I know what I want, what to look forward to.

I started in the program as a trainee and became a counselor. I'm hoping to become a supervisor and further my education and be somebody, so I can teach my kids to be the same way I am. I hope that everything will work out for the better for the youths, because they are the ones who are going to lead us.

Most of the adults sit behind desks or work at whatever type of job they have. They don't go into institutions and see what's going on, what happens to people who are in there. It's a bad situation when you have to take someone that never went through the system and put them through the system. Either the kids don't come out of the system, because they wind up killing themselves, getting raped, or whatever, or it affects them mentally and they don't come out the same person.

84

WILMA GARCIA: I have been in the Ching-A-Ling Community Development Corporation for over three years. I was attending a Catholic high school. In school, the Ching-A-Lings had a reputation for being a bad street gang. I approached some of the sisters who were members of the Ching-A-Lings, and we became good friends. I began to understand that the Ching-A-Lings were not what they were saying in school.

The Ching-A-Lings are a gang and also a family, a family consisting of different denominations and races interested in bettering their community and themselves. I didn't know what I was seeking. With time, I learned that I was seeking the closeness of a family. Coming from a family of only one parent, I never experienced the closeness of a big family, like the Ching-A-Lings have. I was able to join the Ching-A-Lings and help with their program.

The Ching-A-Lings taught me how important an education is and how it could benefit the family. I graduated from Aquinas High School in 1979, with a four-year scholarship to Fordham University. I am working as a counselor with the Ching-A-Lings.

Many of the youths in our programs are in many ways the same. They need counseling by counselors with whom they can identify. Being from the community and knowing the needs of the youths, we are able to bring them a real feeling of caring and understanding.

I am working for my bachelor of arts in sociology. I am confident that the work the Ching-A-Lings are doing is a worthwhile project. I'm proud of it, proud of its limited success.

ROBERT AGUAYO: I work for El Centro del Pueblo, a community center in Los Angeles. I'm going to give you a brief history of my background. I am the youngest of five brothers. All of my brothers and my mother were in gangs. We had four different gangs represented in the family, and we had a lot of fights in the home because of the gangs. Because I was the youngest, I had a chance to see all the problems and all the mistakes of my brothers. I had a brother who was into drugs. Another brother shot three people and was going to go to prison. Another brother was so hardheaded that if you said one little word, he would beat you—and usually he would beat me.

I was growing up in this area, with the Diamond Street gang, one of the oldest gangs in Los Angeles (it started in the late 1940s). I saw a lot of killings, stabbings, fighting, and police harassment—a lot of people beating policemen, a lot of police beating people. I was affected by this, as anybody would be. There is no way you're going to become a perfect person after watching all this happen.

By the time I was eleven, my mom was already labeling me a gang member. Society has a habit of doing that, labeling somebody something. Society not only means teachers, business people, police, but also your parents and your brothers. My brothers were also labeling me a gang member. By the time I was twelve or thirteen, I was participating in gang activities, not heavily, but I was involved in them.

When I was fourteen, my brother was killed by a police officer. He was shot point-blank with a .38 while he was sitting down at a school; the shot blew off half his head. He was shot because he was a gang member—that's the bottom line—the police officer did not like him because he was a gang member. This was the brother who told me to stay away from gangs, although he was in one. His last words were about his gang. That's how dedicated he was to his gang. Yet he was the one telling me to stay away. He was seventeen at the time.

Then his gang, which I also belonged to, looked at me as being just like him. I was to take over what he was doing. Although he was seventeen years old, he was one of the leaders of the young guys. I started influencing people into doing bad things. I was in the ninth grade and had about thirty seventh-graders going around, beating people, anybody I said.

At that time, I was referred to the center where I'm working now, for counseling. I thought these guys would be just another probation department thing. Why would I want these people to counsel me? I'm going to walk in; they're going to read me my regulations, like in probation, and out I go. They'll tell me I can't hang around with these people. I can't carry guns.

There are a lot of people here who were from gangs or who work with gangs. Whenever somebody says that he was a gang member, that means that everyday of his life he was in trouble or being chased or could have been killed. He doesn't have to run down exactly what he did in those times, because everybody knows that a gang member lives a dangerous life everyday of his life.

I went to the center; the people there started counseling me. They started asking me, "What would you like to do? What interests do you have? What don't you like about school? What don't you like about your home? How are people treating you?" At first, I thought they were doing it because that's their job. Then I realized that they were concerned about me. They were telling me, "We want to help you." Whenever I had trouble, I would call them. Even at midnight, one of the counselors would come; that shocked me. These people came from their beds just to help me.

For a period of time, the counseling was going in one ear and coming out the other. You cannot help anybody unless he wants to be helped. The counselors were telling me all these things, but I didn't want to listen. It wasn't my time. I was saying to myself that I was going because I had to go. Then they got me involved in another group. I was a representative of that group from my gang. At their meetings they would use my potential to be a gang leader or a leader in the community to influence a lot of people.

One of the bad things about those meetings was that I always opened my mouth about what was happening with my gang; so I was put on the blacklist. When you're put on the blacklist, you can be killed—and, most of the time, you are. Luckily, I had a brother in the gang that wanted to get me; he solved that for me. He was up in the ranks. He told the gang to leave me alone; it took him a lot of explaining of why I was in that group and what the whole thing was about. Some people didn't have any idea of what the group really was.

Through this work, the center realized that I could influence a lot of people, that I had potential to influence not only my gang, but other people, people just getting into a gang.

I was also involved, through my program, in a wilderness survival program, consisting of four different gangs. Two members of each gang would backpack in the Grand Canyon in summer. It's very hot there. There was no incident between the four gangs, though they were rival gangs. From that experience, I met one of my best friends, who was from a rival gang; to this day, he is a very close friend. That influenced me a lot. I had never liked that gang, I never liked that guy. All of a sudden, we sat down in the Grand Canyon, and we started discussing some of the problems we had in Los Angeles. We started coming out with some feelings—we would never do this back in Los Angeles—about what would scare us, some of the things that our home boys did that we would never tell because we wanted to make our gang look like the strongest. We shared a lot of experiences. My friend grew from that, too. He's away from his gang now.

After that, I did a little bit of peer counseling with my center. The center put me on a youth advisory committee. I had a voice in what happened at our center. I was exposed to some of the working elements in the community. They showed me some opportunities that I could get into, besides going to prison or being busted or getting killed.

They got me enrolled in college, something I never thought I would do. In the eleventh grade, my teacher told me to drop out of school and get a laborer's job. He said I was too dumb. Now I'm going for my bachelor of arts in psychology. I found that I liked college. It was something that I wanted to do, not something somebody was pushing me into.

I am the senior youth counselor. I'm only twenty-one; I'm young but I know what I'm doing. I've been there. I know the other side of it, also. We have to get the people from the community involved, not only because they know the area and what's happening, but because we can teach them the other side of it: how to run programs, what people to meet, the business side of it. With those two elements, they can be successful.

Society labels people. When I was involved in a gang, people used to call me *achollo*. Achollo meant a *parchuko* (gangster). Everybody has heard of a zoot suit: that was a parchuko. It was the symbol of how people thought that were in gangs. They say achollo means a gang member, somebody who starts trouble. That's the main line: a troublemaker, somebody who's going to kill somebody any day now. It's better to put him away, they think.

I had a twenty-minute argument with a parent about that. When I started doing pretty well—I got on my feet, I started taking control of my life—people started saying, "Robert is not achollo any more. He is not a gang member." I'd say, "What do you mean I'm not achollo, I'm not a gang member? What do you mean by that?" "You're not doing this and this," they'd say. I'd say, "What do you mean? Do you mean that achollo means a troublemaker?" They said, "No, it means a gang member." I said, "Yes, but there are gang members that do good."

I'm not against breaking up gangs, because I think everybody has their own little gang. But, we can use gang members to do positive things. When someone is doing negative things, he's a gang member, he's bad news. Once he starts doing good, he's not seen as a gang member. A kid doesn't want to be isolated from his gang, so he doesn't want to do anything good. He wants to be recognized as a gang member; he wants to be a part of the group. He knows if he does something good, all of a sudden his friends are going to say, "What's wrong—what are you doing?" The youths want to keep that identity, but they also ant to do something good. That's why, when you have all the gangs doing something good, everybody wants to be a part of it.

The main thing about us is that we are doing our services, and that's the main point of this whole thing.

SGT. JAMES HARGROVE, New York City Police Department: Unlike the stories that you've heard earlier, about the successes of your groups, I sit here wearing two hats. I am here as an employee of the New York City Police Department. I'm a sergeant, and I supervise a unit in the youth aid division called the street gang unit. The other hat that I wear is that of chairman of the National Black Police Association, with eighty-three chapters throughout the United States, chapters like Delaware County, the Hartford Guardians, the Guardians of New York City, and the Philadelphia Guardian Civic League. In every city talked about today, we have a chapter.

Around 1971, the New York City Police Department found that there was a tremendous resurgence of youth gangs in the city. In 1972, Pat Murphy, then police commissioner in New York City, and Ben Ward, then deputy police commissioner and now correctional commissioner for the New York City Department of Corrections, started two programs to deal with the youth gangs. One was a gang task force, with uniformed patrols specifically assigned to bust gangs.

They didn't have much success, so they decided to start an intelligence division that dealt specifically with gangs. That's where I came in. I was assigned to the Brooklyn unit, for a lot of obvious reasons. One of the biggest reasons was that not many bosses wanted the unit in the first place. Nobody wanted to deal with the problem. Intelligence work in police departments across the country means surveillance, sneaky pictures, wiretaps, the whole gamut of the superspy.

I didn't see it that way in my unit. My unit went another route in Brooklyn. I met some resistance. However, nobody else wanted the job; so it wasn't a matter of telling me to get out and go back to patrol. I handpicked the personnel in my unit. I came up with twelve former gang members, guys who lived in Brooklyn and grew up in Brooklyn and knew Brooklyn. My philosophy with the gang unit was that we were not going to sneak around; we were going to walk right up to the kids. We wanted to talk to them, to find out what their problems were. This was a big mistake. When we started talking to kids, we found out what their problems were, but nobody would help us solve their problems.

We had problems like police officers acting like another gang. In other words, in my sector, you don't wear your colors; you're on my turf. Cops were snatching hats, urinating in them, stealing jackets. We had an incident that was investigated, where a clubhouse was burned down shortly after two police officers left the building. So we found that we had problems with the police department acting more like gang members than the gang members; that natural conflict put us in the middle. My unit in Brooklyn became the least popular in the police department.

We started telling the kids about getting summer jobs. Instead of demonstrating and bringing down a hundred cats, we told them to get ten kids with voter registration cards and start waving them and start voting. The Ching-A-Lings started carrying blank forms for voter registration cards in their saddlebags. Again, that was not our job, allegedly.

One of the biggest problems that I've had with the police department and the criminal justice institution is their philosophy of breaking up gangs. As a minority member, I find that the biggest problems we have as minorities is uniting, getting together, moving together. I saw the gangs as a positive thing. If you could take three kids and direct five hundred, it was worth keeping them together. If you could take those three and push them in the right direction, you would only have to deal with three. That's when I hooked up with ICRY, and I found that the group was talking about doing the same thing.

My first knowledge of ICRY came with a phone call. Somebody asked me if I had any knowledge of it, and I said no. I was sent the yellow sheet on a few individuals, indicating that this must be a dangerous group, because of the leadership. However, we've developed a firm working relationship with ICRY.

My unit in Brooklyn and the youth division in New York City are slated to be eliminated altogether. The New York City Police Department has put a bill before the city council that would effectively eliminate a youth division in the New York City Police Department. The department's philosophy is that if you're a criminal, regardless of your age, you're dealt with by the force; you go to jail. There should be no specialization—every police officer is a youth officer. We're in a lot of trouble, I think. That was one of the first cutbacks proposed. That is because youths don't vote and they have no power in government agencies.

In New York City, we have 127 active gangs, with another 144 groups under investigation. By "under investigation," I mean that we have heard that there is a group, but we have not got the manpower to go out there and find out if, in fact, it does exist. A good 60 percent of the 144 do exist; so we're talking about some 20,000 kids who are in organized gangs in the city of New York.

I'd like to get away from the police department aspect and put on the other hat, that of chairman of the National Black Police Association (NBPA). Our eighty-three organizations throughout the country were formed basically for our own self-interest. We needed promotions; we wanted to get into radio cars; we wanted to get work in the detective divisions. To fight the discrimination in the departments, we formed a self-serving organization. We did not have the backing of the Fraternal Order of Police, the Police Benevolent Associations, the traditional police unions; we were not really interested in what they were interested in anyway.

We have found, from hard knocks, that our biggest supporter is the black community. As a result, we are making a valid attempt to get all our chapters to work closely with community-based organizations that exemplify the goals and objectives of the NBPA. We hope that, when

I leave here, some of our chapters will be working a lot closer with youth-identified organizations.

We're going through a transition with black police officers in the country. We still have the mentality, the "Hollywood image," of police departments. We still have black police officers aspiring to be the image of what TV has made them. But I think that we are coming along. I'm proud that I am a police officer and that I'm in this company and accepted. [Applause.]

James Hargrove,
New York City Police Department

Albert (Crazy Cat) Mejias,
Inner City Roundtable of Youth (ICRY)

Sister M. Isolina Ferré,
Dispensario San Antonio, Inc.

Discussion

ROBERT WOODSON, American Enterprise Institute: This morning we would like to probe deeper into some of the issues that were raised yesterday, principally by Tee Rodgers and some of the other young people. Why would young people like yourselves, who have exercised a lot of influence, enjoyed a lot of respect and authority among your peers and gangs, why would you give that up for programs like SEY YES, like the Youth Identity Project, like the House of Umoja, like Youth in Action, and all the other programs represented here?

We can begin by having the young people give some serious thought to that and perhaps discuss it with the rest of the group. This is important, because traditional programs—with their elaborate bureaucratic structures, with all their millions of dollars being spent to deal with these problems—have not been effective. What we are seeing here is the difference in what these programs are doing versus what traditional programs are doing.

Then, after discussion of that topic, we want to ask each person in the room who is a member of an organization, both the young people and the adults, to think about his two most pressing needs and to tell us why they are so significant. Then Bob Hill, director of research, at the National Urban League, and I will discuss with you the whole issue of evaluation, the whole issue of assessment, with some discussion of how one begins to evaluate and assess the effectiveness of organizations at the local level.

In the afternoon, we want to talk about the relationship of these organizations to certain environmental or external factors. What is it like, operating in the environment of some of these urban centers, dealing with the police? That is an easy question, easy in terms of identifying what some of the problems are, because we have touched upon them and because we come in contact with the police. What about some of the rules and regulations that you have to deal with on a daily basis that say, for instance, in the city of Philadelphia, that in order for anyone to run a program for young people, whether you are getting government funds or not, you have to have a master's degree in social work, or you have to have so much floor space, so much candlelight power, all the various rules and regulations, the reporting requirements?

In other words, what happens to you when you apply for money and you get funds from some of these established organizations? What are some of the problems that are created? To what extent do the funds cause conflicts? Sister Fattah touched upon that, as did others, talking about obtaining money from some of these sources with all their elaborate reporting requirements and the stress caused within the group.

What kinds of problems does this create for you, and how have you coped with these problems? You have an organization that is based upon volunteers and a feeling of family and closeness and cohesiveness— and this is why the young people came to you. But what happens when you begin to move toward a bureaucracy with all those requirements? What is it that you have to give up, and are willing to give up? What impact does that have on your effectiveness and credibility with young people? These may not be questions that we can fully answer here, but at least we have to ask these questions.

I will make a brief presentation about what the federal government has in mind over the next few years in the whole area of juvenile justice and delinquency prevention and what it has been funding and what its policy priorities are. Then I would like to solicit your response to what the federal agencies are doing, to what extent these policies are supportive of what you are doing.

Tee, a person like you has maybe 8,000 people behind him. You can go into the bathroom at a high school and, within five minutes, have people tell you a number of things going on in the school and collect some money; you have that kind of power, authority, and respect on the street. When you met V. G. Guinses and some of the people in the program, you began to rethink and maybe change the way you used your time and your influence toward something positive? Why?

DARRYL (TEE) RODGERS, SEY YES: Two things: the first one is that you and your beliefs and your values change; life becomes a strange and confusing game. The second one is opportunity.

People around the nation, people around the world, are afraid of what they do not understand. When you understand exactly what it is all about, then you say, "It's not like I thought at all." In the ordeal of growing up, you say, "It was like this at the beginning, but it is not like this now." You need the opportunity to say, "I cut, I bleed, I cry, I die, I love, I laugh, I feel just like everybody else." This need is misunderstood by people who do not know what is going on. They do not get an understanding until it's a one-on-one confrontation, without hostility, without remorse, just talking about whatever you want to talk about.

When I started off, I had a constant struggle within myself over Blackstone love, which means that I love everybody who is with me, and I don't like anybody else. With that concept, how can I love one brother and kill another? These are the things that hurt me, being the leader. It drowned my brain with a constant depression.

I finally got an opportunity to swing around, from the bullet to the ballot, which was the chance that I needed. I would rather die on my feet than live on my knees. You don't have to give me anything. If it comes down to it, I will take it, if I have to. However, if you give me a chance to show what I can do in a progressive manner, then I will do so by myself. If I need any guidance or encouragement, then be there when I need you. Other than that, I am a man, and I can stand on my own two feet.

MR. WOODSON: When you met V.G., what did he say to you? What did he represent to you? How did he provide you with the opportunity? What did V.G. do that impressed you, that made him different from other people who have tried to talk with you, perhaps even your own parents?

MR. RODGERS: It was the final say-so, "If you don't want to do it, don't." V.G. pointed out that all the time he has worked with youngsters, he has never cursed, nor has he physically touched anyone, assaulted anyone, hit anybody. When I first met him, I did not know that, but he has a unique understanding which I hadn't found in anyone who was not from a gang structure. At the confrontation between us, playing mind games with people, he let me play my game, but he also let me know that I could not win, not here. To recapture the situation, I said, if I hook up with your program, then, being from a gang situation, I reject authority as a whole. I don't care whose authority. I don't like it, period. He is authority, because he's in society, in the establishment. Let me find out what is happening. If you are going to give me a job and I am going to work, make me work. He said, "I'm not going to make you do anything. If you want to work, if you want to better yourself, then do so." Again, here was the chance, the opportunity, to show everybody within my community that there are two sides to me. There are two sides to my set, to my club. We don't have to be deviant all the time.

In Los Angeles, once you are labeled as a gang, that is it. As Flint Agosto said, from the time you get into it until the day you die, that is what you will be about. V.G. opened up certain areas, opportunities, and doors for me to get through without getting grabbed by my collar, with people saying, "What are *you* doing here? You can't stick up anything here."

DR. BRIGITTE BERGER, professor of sociology, Smith College: If I understand what it means to be somebody on the street, an important part of it is courage. You are somebody who can take care of himself. People had better watch out before they cross you. You are taking risks. You can take it. All of that is important. Aren't you giving some of this up? Compared with what you did before, isn't what you are doing now a bit colorless, a bit dull?

MR. RODGERS: That's a good question. All over the nation, if you have two grownups, six feet five inches, 280 pounds apiece, and they are arguing whatever they want to argue over, they are not going to come at each other until the police or the umpire gets there. Once the umpire steps in there, one guy says, "I will kill him," but the umpire steps in, and breaks them up. The guy says, "You are lucky the police got here, because I would have torn your head off." See, he doesn't lose anything. He keeps that manly respect. It's not so much courage, as it is respect. In order to get respect, you have to give respect. I would demand respect by any means necessary. As I stand alone, five feet, six inches, 165 pounds, I am nobody. But when I stand here, five feet, six inches and 8,000 strong, then you listen to me.

That is the difference right there. It's not so much courage, as I see, because I have talked with the brothers from around the nation. When we come here, we say, "We have been in situations, and, man, we were scared to death." You do what you have to do. A lot of times in Los Angeles you are forced into situations. We would not even have gotten a gang label if they hadn't shot at us. You learn early. If somebody punches you in your eye, you punch him back, in order to stay on top. This is about respecting us as people.

V. G. GUINSES, SEY YES: In Los Angeles, the key thing is getting respect. The geographic location of gangs in Los Angeles is widespread, but the gang territories are maybe one block or two blocks apart. Tee Rogers mentioned about respect, about courage. When a young guy in Los Angeles can walk through other neighborhoods without being approached or jammed or jumped on, he has the key, respect.

There is a variety of answers to Mr. Woodson's question, because each individual is different. I am dealing with close to twenty-five different gang groups. Whatever affected Tee in coming to me or getting involved, I couldn't use that same approach on another young guy, because each one is different, for example the females we work with.

The key thing in Los Angeles is respect. In L.A., a gang will kill you for respect. They will fight behind respect. And they are recognized. If a kid is only three feet tall, if he has the respect to walk in another territory without getting jumped because of doing something positive, that is more respect than he received when he was in the gang fighting. Tee can pull in more groups than Blackstones. They respect him, and they come here for help, also. That's such a big thing in L.A., respect. One of the worst killings we had was a bus driver, killed because he disrespected one of the smallest young kids on the bus; so they offed him.

But you have other young people around here; their answers may be different. If you have three kids in a family, your kids are different.

MR. RODGERS: You become more colorful, because you have respect among all the gangs. Once you are a gang member, you fight in the street, and everybody from every corner knows who has respect and who doesn't have respect, plus you get more respect because you are doing things in a positive way. You can relate to the corner and the community. You wouldn't be losing your respect; you would be gaining more respect, because you can deal with them with both aspects.

ROBERT (FAT ROB) ALLEN, the House of Umoja: In Philadelphia, wherever I go, they know me. If all of you in this room was from a different corner, you would know me. You would know that I am going to hurt something. You might know the other guy is going to be there to back me up, but you know when I come there, I am coming there to hurt something. This wins respect at one level, but if you have respect from all the gangs in the city, and start doing positive things in the community, you have the respect of the community. That way you have the respect of the community and the gangs, and you can deal better.

That is just like the police officers. They will try to pull your respect down, but how can they pull your respect down? You have respect with the corners in the community. In 1977, I was shot by a cop because of misidentification. It took getting shot by a cop to get some credit for halting gang wars in the city. The cops try to take your respect, but they can't. The only way they can take your respect is by breaking you, and there are not many black males they are going to break.

You ask what positive thing do you do, that has more clout, more influence, than being able to hurt somebody? When I walk in this room and everybody in here is getting ready to gang-war, and when I leave this table, everybody here decides they want peace, that's respect. You don't lose respect. What you gain is self-pride.

SISTER FALAKA FATTAH, the House of Umoja: Maybe I should add a little prayer. When we had the gang conference, the two things that came out, that the brothers said they wanted, were, first, respect and, second, jobs. In terms of trying to go from respect to jobs, what we discussed was how do you get respect. The respect that had been gained at that point was on a physical level.

In order to get to the jobs, we have to talk about this transference. How can you get a job if people are scared to death of you? People don't want to come near you. People don't want to be with you if they are afraid of you. You have to make that transference.

The other thing that came through clearly was the fact that this society has taken away from black men and other minorities the respect of manhood. They are put in a position where they have to take from others, take what other people have because others run things. Other people have hotels; they run big businesses. They are constantly trying to make a black man less than what he is. They put him in a position of having to gain respect on another level.

The brothers at the House of Umoja have the most respect in the street, first of all, because they have earned it in the street and, second, because they were able to go out and bring in the other corners to make peace. They were not considered cowards. They are not considered cowards now. They are still leaders.

MR. ALLEN: The respect that I have for Sister Falaka comes from trust. When I can trust somebody, I can respect that person. If I am sitting in jail, I know that she is home, she is taking care of business for me. I know that she is going to be on the case, she is going to be down at city hall. When you trust somebody, it takes a lot off your mind. When you are from a gang and get out of being from a gang and you start doing positive things in the community, the gangs even respect you more. A lot of people think we are ignorant, but I have found that most gang members are intelligent.

You can have respect in a lot of ways, just like when they see little write-ups in the paper about us. That is something big to them, because they are saying this is somebody who made it, and they haven't forgotten us. When you make it and forget them, that is when they lose their respect for you.

DR. BRIGITTE BERGER: If it is that clear, why doesn't it happen everywhere?

100

MR. RODGERS: There are different levels of respect. People don't respect our communities. You have a dual problem. If there is a lot on my block, for instance, people throw garbage on it. The trash man doesn't take it away. I call downtown. The man hangs up on me. He doesn't respect me. That means that something has to be done.

A lot of times the people who will understand much easier are people who understand the general concept of being respected. That is something that the brothers have done. I say, "Let's go downtown and see if we can get it straightened out." We go downtown sometimes, and I say, "We have been calling down here, and you hung up on Mrs. Jones, and somebody said you said something that wasn't nice. We would appreciate it if you got that straightened out."

Then people see the trash truck come down there the next morning or that day, before we get back, and clean the lot or pick up the trash; that makes the entire community feel better. It gives other corners something to look at. They say, "Those dudes are taking care of their neighborhood."

The other part of respect is your word, no matter what that word is. If you tell somebody, "If you don't stop something, I am going to come down on you." People understand that if you come down there, you aren't going to be playing with them. Then you don't have to do a lot of things.

It took the people who had the respect of the corners and the gangs to communicate that there is going to be a change, and explain why that change is necessary, that respect was not going to be dropped, but that we are going to take it to a higher level. We aren't going to stop running our turf. We want to run our turf and make it safe, make it sound. If somebody takes somebody's pocketbook and we want the pocketbook back, the pocketbook comes back.

These are the types of things, the transference, whereby everybody feels better than they did, rather than when you kill somebody and that creates some kind of grief. You know how you felt when somebody killed your brother. You know how you felt when somebody shot at you. You ask, "Why don't we take this whole thing to a higher level? Why don't we, instead of attacking ourselves, attack items?"

DAVID FATTAH, the House of Umoja: To add to that, suppose you are a leader of a gang, and people in the community, your neighborhood, know that you, as the leader, control a certain body of young men who do a lot of vandalism. The leader might say, "To gain the respect of the community, maybe we should have a cleaned-up neighborhood run by the gang." This has been used in a lot of cities. The gang itself will call the mayor or call the street department and say, "We need so many bags, so many bushels. We are going to take care of our turf."

The leader is saying to other members in the gang, "One of the ways we can get the police off our backs and get people to look at us more in a positive way is do a project or a program." Doing that, cleaning up the block and sweeping for a whole week, gives the community and other people who read the newspaper and watch television a more positive look at the gang as something positive now.

They are helping and cleaning the community. Through that, they regain more respect. Gangs in other areas say, "If they can clean their area, we need basketball courts in our area." These are some of the positive things that they might do to gain more respect from the communities beyond respect within their own gang.

NIZAM FATAH, ICRY: Once someone asked Louis Armstrong, "What's jazz?" He said, "If I have to try to explain it to you, you will never know."

We're talking about credibility. How can Tee go from one place to another and keep his level of respect? People feel that he has a certain capability—he is able to take care of himself. He is able to relate. He is moving into another direction, and everybody wants to go with him. They want to know can he be trusted enough to carry them in the direction with him as he moves along.

We put together a community anticrime program in New York; it was the first time that this had been done in the city. We brought together three groups—the Savage Riders, Ching-A-Lings, and the Five Percent—in a patrol situation in what was called Dopeville, U.S.A., right in central Harlem.

Nobody wanted to go for that particular program. We tried it for ten weeks to see if we could do anything. Naturally, the citizens couldn't handle the junkies in that area or the crime or anything concomitant.

There had been all these little patrols all over the city. We had been reading about them. One little high school group got together and put a bunch of boy scouts on bicycles, with walkie-talkies. They got about a half a block. They didn't have their bicycles or walkie-talkies or anything left.

We brought in these three gangs. People were still wearing their patches, their colors. They all had jackets. Everybody knew who they were. Looking at them, the junkies knew that there were going to be some serious confrontations. The junkies tried them all kinds of ways. They wouldn't try them physically, but they started saying things like, "We expected more of you guys than this, to try to clean up the neighborhood," and, "We think this is wrong, you guys being a part of the police department."

We had to figure out how to approach this without looking like another arm of the law. We decided to make it the law that everybody in the inner city understands, an intimidation without any type of violence or vigilante action. We never had any confrontations. We are the only group existing today in New York City that was successful with this type of a project. From that, the cash program became pretty well funded through community anticrime funds, just from our efforts. Probably, that was the major success. The program was known all over the country, in fact, even in Germany and other places, because we were successful with this particular function.

At the same time, this program created such a controversy that the officials decided to move us out and bring back the same guys on the bicycles and whatnot. We even had the senior citizens march on city hall; they wanted to know why we weren't going to continue the services that we had done in the community. People were worried about how raggedy the kids looked, how they liked to dress. Flint has chains on, from his bike and whatnot. We had a meeting with the senior citizens in the area. We said, "These people want us to put on shirts and ties"—which they did. "The Urban Coalition wants us to wear shirts and ties while we are escorting you back and forth." One little old lady—she was ninety-four years old—jumped up and said, "I want them looking just like that when they walk me someplace."

It's a kind of respect that is difficult to explain. Respect is a word like love. Everybody is always trying to explain it. You don't know what it is, but you recognize it when you see it, or should.

It's a credibility factor. When we go out to recruit, I do that, but basically it's Flint, or he sends somebody from the club. We may not even be on good terms with the other group, but generally you walk in there, knowing exactly the assessment of the needs because they are the same needs that you have. The other guys know this is a capable guy. He is a straight-up-and-down kind of a brother, dealing with the same type of problems. He is telling you something you can get out of this, what we are trying to get out of it; neither one of us can do it alone. This is what bands us together, what keeps that type of credibility.

DR. BRIGITTE BERGER: I think the idea you have about transference is an important one. The transference is at first geared toward the leaders of the gangs. Is that correct?

SISTER FATTAH: The transference wasn't intentionally geared toward the leaders of the gangs. It has happened that way. The House of Umoja attracted the leaders of the gangs.

DR. BRIGITTE BERGER: Once you have that, aren't there really two kinds of transferences going on, not one? You talk about the transference from one to the other, but you have two steps there. The first is the transference from a violent gang to a nonviolent gang. Once they are in that nonviolent group, something else is happening, and that's the important thing.

MR. NIZAM FATAH: The violence is still there. Nobody has exchanged that. The brothers are gang-warring for the community. That is the difference. They are using the same intensity to fight for what they believe is rightfully theirs. People are not shooting one another, because they have changed their target. A person is in the leadership of a battle, because he is the best at it, in that one arena. You have to take that same leadership into the next arena.

We are gang-warring for jobs, because we have brothers in prison. When they come out, if they don't have a job, they have to make a choice between the opportunity to make it legitimately and the opportunity to make it illegitimately. If you take away one option, what do you have left? The jobs are important.

DR. BRIGITTE BERGER: Tee earlier identified his change in personal values and an opportunity to advance. Did Tee give any consideration to his role as a leader and the responsibility that he had to those 8,000 behind him?

MR. RODGERS: I had to consider my role as a leader. The governing body was set up, as most clubs around the nation are set up. If you kill the head, then the body can't function.

What they don't realize is that Rob Allen can call the shots from inside the jailhouse. Flint can call shots from anywhere in the world, if he has to. I stayed in the house for two and a half years, because I made the ten most-wanted gang leader list in south central Los Angeles; I called the shots from my telephone.

With this in mind, I can't say we are not going to be Blackstones, but we are all going to be Christian Blackstones. I have the power. It comes to a governing body. All the heads sit down, and we talk it out. Ninety-nine percent of the time, I went over the problem of the situation so much that they trust my decisions. There may be some opposition, but after it's talked out and worked out, they say, "We'll try it at least, if nothing else."

I'm not alone. I have thought about everybody. Rob Allen made a good point about holding life and death in your hands. They say, "Here they come. They have guns. We aren't going to run."

JOHN (FLINT) AGOSTO, the Ching-A-Ling Development Corporation: When a child comes to me, right away I put myself in his shoes. I look at him and say, "Wow, that's me twenty years ago." That gives me an advantage, because I can relate to the youth. Whatever problems he is going through, I went through them. In my time, there were no solutions. Now we have a few.

I was shown a film made about Rahway prison in New Jersey, called *Scared Straight*. After I viewed it, I told the interviewers that the film was bull. When any of my children get arrested, before he even hits the court, the prison knows he is coming. The underground word gets out quickly. "A Ching-A-Ling is coming to a jail. Take care of him."

If you're a Savage Rider or belong to a gang in New York City, if it's a respected gang and any of your members gets arrested, the jail is notified right away: "One of the brothers is coming. Take care of him."

That's why I mentioned the film. All the kids in the film were individuals, kids with their own personal problems. They didn't belong to any sect or party. Of course, that is the treatment they get in jail.

If you belong to an organization, you have less fear of going to jail. I try not to tell this to my members, but they understand it, because most of them have been in jail. We try to put the fear of jail in kids, but it doesn't work a lot of times.

MR. NIZAM FATAH: Last summer, some kids who were what we call unaffiliated just hung out at the office. They were into a lot of things, doing a lot of things. Some of them hadn't been to jail, and they didn't have that kind of cover or protection. Practically all of them said, "I can see all this happening." They said, "That is one of the reasons why this time if I get busted and I think I am going up there, I am going to resist arrest. I am going to shoot somebody."

That was one of the reactions to that film, and I have heard this in a lot of places. That is what that kind of film does. In fact, we wrote about it in our newsletter, and we were trying to be nice about it. We used all the euphemisms we could. But that film is terrible. Every day we get a letter from some prison that wants to hook up with us, for us to come in there; it wants to scare somebody straight. I am always saying, "Send me something and let me see what your approach to this particular thing is."

It winds up being the same thing. In the first place, trying to scare people is not going to stop anybody from going to jail. They are not stealing because they want to or they have a choice. Whatever they are into, it is something that they have to do one way or another, unless this society opens up something a little different for them. I think this is a terrible film.

MR. RODGERS: In dealing with youth fights, I can't go to my corner or any other corner and say, "Hey, look, don't fight these guys." I have to say this: "If you all can talk it out, talk it out, but if you can't talk it out, then you have got to protect yourself."

You can't leave people hanging on the line, saying "It's cool. They ain't fighting no more." Then, when you leave, they blow their brains out. You have to tell them, "If you can't talk to them, then they have got to defend themselves." That is the last alternative. I am going to tell them to protect themselves. I am not going to leave my homies [friends] or nobody else hanging. When I give my word on something, my word means something. You have to be careful how you deal with them. I know how I would feel if somebody came and said, "Don't fight." Then when he leaves, I am lying down shot with somebody dead.

I always tell the brothers, "Look, hey, if the brothers don't want to listen, then you all go ahead, do what you have to do." We had an incident when some brothers wanted to fight. The other brothers didn't want to fight. One of the homies had been shot, so he decided he didn't want to fight. The corner said it wouldn't fight. The other guys, since they shot somebody, wanted to fight. We went to the table, and we couldn't resolve it. They shot fifteen people in two weeks. Then, the brothers were ready to sit down and rap. I said, "We could have done this before you all got shot up."

When you are dealing with them, you have to be honest and tell them, "Don't do it if you can, but if you have to defend yourself, then you have to defend yourself."

MR. DAVID FATTAH: They used to have this ad; it would say, "Would you buy a used car from Richard Milhous Nixon?" At that time he was president of the United States. Either the person would come flat out and say no or would have to think about it. In other words, people didn't trust him, so they didn't respect the guy.

If you take a gang, most people think that a gang is ruled by fear or terror. Maybe that's true for people outside the gang, but every organization works the same. There is not a great deal of difference between a gang organization and a military situation, a political situation, or a community situation. The organization is going to try to survive and reach its objectives. We have only two things going for us out here. We have our pride, and we have each other, friends.

This is the main ingredient in getting things done. You don't want people to disrespect you. You don't want people to say, "Joe said something, you can't believe him. Joe is a notorious liar. He may not show." One of the main things that happened with the brothers in our particular situation is they took the position that their word is their bond. If they say something, that's it. This is what enforces things.

If you say something, you give your word; if you break it, then you are held up for ridicule. Your own homie is turning back on you, because you bring disgrace on the corner. You bring disgrace on everybody around you, on your lady. They say, "Hey, man, this is a jive dude. He can't keep his word."

This enables people to overcome some heavy barriers. Once they said, "If you don't cross Market Street, then everything is all right." You expect that to carry. They will test each other on that. You say, "Well, let me see where his heart is, let's see if this is real." You would look around, try to see if this is going to be the way or not.

One of the things that always amused me is that we would go to politicians sometimes, and we would ask them about jobs. They would look us dead in the face, eyeball-to-eyeball contact. They would say, "You have got it. Bring three of them or four of them down here tomorrow morning at 10:00. Don't be late, and you are all going to have some jobs." We would be down there maybe at 9:30. Everybody is getting up early, rushing down there. Guess what, man, there are no gigs [jobs].

If somebody said we stopped gang-warring, did he mean it? As far as I was concerned, that was settled. We would talk to the next person about whether he was going to stop, because he didn't want to be embarrassed. He didn't want to be dishonored.

The problem we ran into was not with the gangs keeping their word. If they hadn't kept their word, in Philadelphia, it would still be gang-warring tough. The problem was the politicians. It was even teachers. A teacher would say, "Yeah, well, look, Dave, I will tell you what. That kid is kind of rough, man, but we are going to let him back in school, if he comes in every day on time, and he wears blue sneaks." Okay, man, give this guy some blue sneaks, get him in there on time. The next thing you hear, "I am sorry, Dave, I didn't know he had done this." This is the crux to peace anywhere, or war anywhere. If you say there is going to be war, then everybody takes cover. By the same notion, if you come out and say there is going to be peace, then you are supposed to be able to go see your girlfriend and walk around the corner and put your pistol away.

We have never told anybody to throw a pistol away, because this is a dangerous society. Gangs are not the major threat to people in this society. We tell them put your pistol away. This whole country is built on the fact that you are supposed to have a cannon or gun somewhere, not that I do, of course. In fact, that is the First Amendment, the right to bear arms. When they were putting this country together, somebody was anticipating some trouble.

We began to take the brothers out of context. Another problem we had was with the press. They are another bunch of folks who used to have a little trouble getting the facts straight. In this situation, in peace, you have to get the facts straight. If the guy means Market Street, he can't say Chestnut Street. If you put in the paper he said Chestnut Street, somebody can get hurt, because a lot of people believe exactly what they see in the paper. I have seen that go down a lot. If somebody is misquoted, all hell breaks loose. By the time the smoke clears and you clean up what is left, the guy said, "Oh, I thought he said this other thing."

The social workers are famous for that. They come into the neighborhood telling somebody some lie and wonder why nobody will listen to them. I have heard of social workers being gagged and tied and put on a bus—and they were fortunate—and shipped downtown.

It all goes back to truth. Some truths are universal, or at least Shakespeare said so; the Bible says things are universal. There are certain characteristics that human beings have, that are universal; one of them is integrity. If a dude's word is good, you can go anywhere on that dude's word. It's like having a credit card. It's as if you have an American Express card. You go in a store and show it; you are supposed to get some goods, and that is what it's about.

When we don't deal with the brothers like brothers, we are going to take them out of context and make them different. I see newspaper articles calling people animals. Animals—what did they do, bite somebody? That is why it's not only respect among ourselves we need. We want respect around the table, across the board. We want respect from everybody, from researchers, foundations, government, everybody. That isn't happening in America—or you wouldn't have an Equal Rights Amendment. Apparently, some men somewhere must not be respecting the women, or we wouldn't need it.

When we can focus on that, we can start sitting down and getting into it. Then I know that when you come at me with how you feel or what the situation is, we can put it on the table and turn it around. Then I can say either that I can deal with that or I can't deal with that, and we will all walk away from that table feeling more like men and women. That is where that other layer comes, that good feeling you get when you know that when you pick up the phone, or you go somewhere, and you open your mouth, people will say, "Okay. I know that is the rap."

DR. BRIGITTE BERGER: I want to ask again about the violence still there. It was said that the violence is important in the struggle for getting jobs. What kind of jobs are they and how do you use the violence?

MR. RODGERS: Brothers, gangdoms, everybody in America wants the same thing. They want some cash in their pocket. They want a job they can go to, knowing they are going to get paid and have some advancement in it. They want a Seville. They want a house somewhere. This is what everybody wants. It is not that our desires are different. When people don't get what they want, they get violent, they get hostile, they get to be hard.

If you come on your job and somebody doesn't come through right, you might give him some violent body language. You might not actually act it out all the way, but you are going to send off a violent vibration, which is the first step to hurting somebody.

When people don't have gigs and they have to sit around and put their hands out like children, though they are grown men, and they get a welfare check or something, then they begin to get hostile. They don't want to hear a whole lot of crap. This is where violence and joblessness go together.

If a person doesn't have a job, sooner or later he is going to get in trouble. If you mess with somebody or the money isn't right, you are going to get hurt. The U.S. government is the same way. If you mess with those oil wells, you are going to get hurt. This is the way this system is. There is no difference in what we want, from what you want, your cash. The difference is only in the differences that we make among ourselves.

SISTER FATTAH: In terms of how I know the violence is still there, we have been working, trying to build a boys' town for twelve years. When we show our plans to different people, they think it is just brick and mortar; we try to explain that the building of the boys' town is a monument to the brothers' word. When I make a presentation, people assume that I am a good sister who wants to do something for children. But when people interfere with the dream of getting the boys' town built, the brothers from the street will come in and say, "Who is standing in the way? Who needs to be offed (killed)?" They don't want to know all the dialogue that went on and how come so-and-so said they are going to do something and then did not want to do it. If they read something in the paper where somebody is not being responsive, sooner or later they show up. Sometimes we haven't seen them in years. They will just show up at the House and ask, "What is the holdup?" They are not playing. I try to communicate that, when I am dealing with people so that they understand that it needs to be built. If they don't have something that says here is our monument to keeping our word, this is what it is about, then it means that you have disrespected all that bloodshed, disrespected all those brothers who said that they wanted to do something and did it in a positive manner.

You can't equate this project with a recreation center. It is not about recreation. What is being said here is how a person feels about something. It's the intensity and what that represents to people. You have all kinds of monuments and statues to other kinds of battles. You have generals up on horses in the middle of a park, because they led a battle and they won. The brothers want that kind of monument at the House of the Umoja. If they don't get it peaceably, they are going to get it any way they have to get it. That's how I know there is still violence.

DR. BRIGITTE BERGER: How do you go about getting the jobs?

SISTER FATTAH: That is the problem, because there are more people who need them than we are able to get them. We are going into business to try to create them.

ROSE NIDIFFER, El Centro del Pueblo: One of the problems that we encounter is that our youths have a hard time understanding the world they live in. Our community is multicultural, with 67 percent being Hispanic. We have local money through our council people. We have $150,000 that goes into our community each year to an agency that is not doing anything. The youths want to know why it is they are getting that money. How do you explain to them, that those people have the councilmen to their house for dinner and things like that? Recently we applied for some money that was allocated for juvenile delinquency through the criminal justice planning office in the city. We are doing all the services in our community as far as working with the youths, the delinquents, the gangs, but we are vocal and we take stands.

CRASH, the Community Resource Against Street Hoodlums, came into our community and did a community sweep. Ten guys committed a crime; thirty guys were arrested; the suspect list had forty-three. They identified them with books. This is the Diamond Street gang. This is the 18th Street gang. This is the Echo Park gang.

They have been stopping our youth at the parks and on the street, photographing them with the gang placard in front of them. The community people came to us. We plugged them into the ACLU (American Civil Liberties Union), and they filed a class action lawsuit to stop this photographing of our youths.

The money didn't go to us because we are vocal and we take stands. It went to an agency that is mostly Anglo; it has no communication whatsoever with the youths in our community. Our youths ask, "Why did they do that? We are the ones doing the services here. Why did they give the money to somebody else?" How do you explain that to them, that it is politics, that it was safe to give it to them, because they are not vocal, they don't take stands? It is difficult to explain it to the young people. You can't even explain it to me.

CARL HARDRICK, SAND: One of the problems in dealing with the gangs is their lack of awareness, their political awareness, of how you make a system work. They knew how their little system worked. You go out there and you do it. But they didn't realize that in the outside world that it just doesn't happen that way or that quickly.

What people are talking about when you get down to the bottom line is the distribution of wealth, from those who have it, to those who do not have it.

When I was interviewing or counseling the gangs, I always knew the bottom line, after everything was said and done, in terms of giving them some sense of direction to go in a positive way, where they can maintain themselves. It was a job. How are you going to come up with the jobs that you need? Others weren't able to make the kind of contacts that you could or have the ability that you had to relate. They knew that others held some upper hand as well, because they had some resources that you need in order to make your thing effective.

You can't get into trade-offs, because when you start trading off, you lose your respect. You lose your respect when you compromise for things that you think are needed; you give up a lot.

A lot of people are saying how it is a struggle. It is a constant struggle. With the sister's boys' town, for instance, the people who are in a position to fund it recognize that. They would hold off and hope that her position would weaken and hope that our ability to deliver or to relate will weaken. The very things that they were asking for did not come from Dr. So-and-so, or did not come from the human resources services within the community. They came from the sister in the community, who saw a need and recognized the abilities and the things that she can do with the young people.

You have many problems as you begin to deal with the young people, and you have many more problems when dealing with the politician, in order to be effective. You can sometimes recognize these things. We recognize on the national level, for example, that it will cost more to run the country from a Defense Department point of view, than it will from a domestic point of view. We understand all the things going down domestically, what's happened in the education system, in the food stamp program, and so forth.

You take that mentality. It's that same mentality locally, too. Why would you hire more policemen when I can get Rob Allen and the rest of the brothers almost to run the city—and we can, pretty much. He is working with the brothers creating all this crime, and he can turn the thing around.

Why don't we contract with Rob rather than contract with the police department? The politician who holds the key, who says who gets what, has the controlling mechanism. The gangs are at one level politically and need to move on another level politically. We do not want to break up gangs. Once you raise the consciousness of the gangs, they have to move from the level of things not happening in city hall to how you make things happen. How do you make them happen? By the vote. How do you get votes? You go out and you register.

In time, you will make things happen. When you talk about jobs, things that the sister needs, things that everybody at this table needs, we do not have the control of those resources or the luxuries, to say, "Okay, let's build a boys' town." When you go to those who have the control, I am not sure whether they want to see that type of thing delivered, because it is not their idea. It didn't come from the university. It came from the community.

DR. PETER BERGER, professor of sociology, Boston University: In coming back to this business of jobs, everything that has been said by the Fattahs, Nizam Fatah, Sister Falaka and David about Hartford has to do with politicians. In other words, what you are saying is that we have a structure here. Let's call it the gang structure. Whether you talk about violence or respect, we know it. We all around this table have a clear idea of what this is. It's a certain way of life with certain values, some of which are very positive.

You are turning this around and translating it into what? Into political clout. Mr. Rodgers used the phrase *bullets to ballots.* Now, that is a big achievement, and that can get you certain kinds of jobs. But what kinds of jobs are they? Jobs that are dependent on politicians—in other words, soft money.

But in the long range, more difficult but also more permanent in its results, is bullets to business or bullets to bottom line in the business sense, that is, to create jobs, to use those same structures that we are talking about here, to create jobs, industry, economic activity, whatever it is, that is not dependent on politicians.

MR. GUINSES: I am speaking for V.G. now, not my organization. Always there are three sides to a story, my side, yours, and the real truth. We are beating around the bush. You have two respects. You have a white respect and you have a black respect. That is what you are dealing with. The jobs you are talking about are limited. Every company I went to, we talked about jobs. What kind of jobs? Peanut money, $2.10 an hour, $2.90 an hour, $3.10 an hour.

You have young people sitting around this room who are experts, who should be on salary. You have people here who are experts, but you don't have respect from the top level to give you that money that you should have, your own money. If you list, on a résumé, what these young people have done in the past year, they have better credentials than any social worker you can think of who deals with your problem. But you do not have respect, because the officials don't figure that you are important. Any time that they can go back and still, after ten years or more, don't give you consideration of your needs, you tell me if you have respect.

You're having a gang problem. You go to a white neighborhood and kill two whites there and you won't have a gang problem. The National Guard will come in and tear you out.

The people you are working with are not working for you. The politicians, the society believe in one thing. There is power in numbers. If you walk downtown, 100,000 strong, and say, "Mr. Carter, we need money for survival; don't cut these programs out; think about our budget and defense," see how you come out.

For years, we have spent billions and billions of dollars on defense, and what have we got in return—$2 million for our youngsters out there putting their lives on the line.

We have been selling gangs, but we haven't been selling that the gangs, the youngsters who keep the neighborhood cool, also keep the white person saying, "That's cool," when he comes into your neighborhood to sell. The youngsters also let the teachers come down into the neighborhood and try to teach your kids. What you should be selling is the whole package, not just the gang, because you don't have to be a gang member to be a victim. Innocent people are being sacrificed. Young guys are out there using their credibility and not getting over.

We are sitting here talking about the difference between respects. There are two respects. There are two justices. If you have money, you don't go to prison. If you don't have money, you will go. This is what we are coming down to. We should get down to reality and move on from there, because we could be here all day talking about respect.

MR. WOODSON: Some of the points that Peter Berger raised, I think are important. We need to discuss them, because even if the federal budget was to continue to expand and expand the social programs and if it wiped out all of the defense budget and put it all in domestic programs, what kind of programs, what kind of money are we talking about?

DR. PETER BERGER: One could put it concretely. Let's take Mr. Fatah's tee shirts. That is a good example of what I am talking about. There are two possible strategies. One is to cajole, intimidate, a bunch of New York politicians to have a program by which some of these kids will make these tee shirts instead of writing graffiti on the subways. That involves the kind of job I think that you are talking about.

The other thing is—I don't know whether it can be done with those tee shirts—the tourist industry. We are talking about selling them to some big-deal designer on Seventh Avenue who will market this all over the country and sell it to a bunch of tourists who come to America and want to take something home. That is a very different proposition, and it's a different strategy, and it's built with a different logic. This second kind, in the long run, is much better, because you are not dependent on city hall, on all these soft structures of the political system.

MR. AGOSTO: Last year, in Washington, I saw some people in the Labor Department, and I threw some new ideas at them. I had my staff, my young staff, do research on motorcycles, because that is my area of expertise. In 1977, the motorcycle industry—European, Japanese, American—sold about 2½ million motorcycles in the United States. The statistics for 1980 are 6 million motorcycles.

We estimate that there are 15 to 16 million motorcycles already in the United States in 1980. There are three mechanics for every 600 motorcycles sold. Only Harley-Davidson, in the last year, started accepting minority people in its training programs.

I approached the people, saying, "Why don't we set up a program where we take these youths and teach them motorcycle skills, motorcycle mechanics?" At the same time, they have to learn how to read and do math, because you have to read a manual. The motorcycle manuals change every year, just like those for cars. New parts are added. New ideas come in. A mechanic must know how to read. That is part of an education for a youth.

I met a lot of people who are going for the idea, but then I ran into the roadblock with the politicians: "We can't give you that type of program because your organization is not accredited. You haven't got teachers with degrees. You just haven't got it." The idea's been shelved.

MR. WOODSON: Peter Berger's point is that that is the reality. The question is, Do you fight for the politician to allow you to work for somebody else and get paid, where that job is dependent upon that politician doing something, or do you fight those politicians for the opportunity to go in business for yourself, to set up your own repair shop, to manufacture your own motorcycles?

A lot of the General Motors mechanics made modifications to their major lines based on what some of these kids did to hot rods. The mechanics came to the kids and found out how the kids modified the engine, the wheel base, the transmission, to do what they wanted, and a lot of those engineers studied what those kids did and then used it.

The issue is, What do you fight for? Do you fight for more soft jobs, more kids being paid by somebody else, that depends upon someone else's good wishes, or do you fight to manufacture your own tee shirts and market them, so that you get the profits?

SGT. JAMES HARGROVE, New York City Police Department: A bigger problem is who do you fight.

MR. AGOSTO: There are mechanics who are capable right now of walking into a place and doing the job. However, they don't have a piece of paper that says they are accredited, so that a company won't accept them. Do they take their fight and bombard the company? Then in comes the government. The police and everybody else are coming in between that company and the Ching-A-Lings. Or do they go to the politicians, or do they go the way that society says they should go? Who do they fight? Do they go down there and bomb the factory? Do they go down there and not let any trucks in? Who do they fight? Or should society say that you are supposed to go see a politician, get somebody as an intermediary, go speak to the company? It's confusing. Who do you fight?

MR. HARDRICK: When we negotiated with Consolidated for the tobacco jobs, the firm was concerned about its costs in terms of the amount of money to bring youngsters up from the south. We were looking at all the jobs that were needed in the fields. At the same time, we went to Aetna Life Insurance, and we said that we recognized Aetna's needs. Aetna said that because of the changes in the job structure, a lot of people went into different job areas, and the firm was looking for certain types of personnel. We're trying to get into Aetna saying, "Look, we can provide the things you need."

The political system controls the education system; one has to feed off the other. Certainly, you can get the youngsters for Aetna, but then you talk about training, because you don't want them in the insurance company washing dishes. You don't want them in something that is going to be nonproductive. We were concerned with bringing the young person in and with middle management not understanding that if he wasn't part of the plan, it would be difficult for him to succeed. Things could stop right there.

There must be constant development. You have to go into the private corporations, because you cannot rely on CETA; CETA changes every which way. LEAA is being phased out. You do need to control the political system. You recognize that in doing interviews in gangs. You have had youngsters who are eighteen years old reading on a second-grade level. How can you stick them into computer programming? You have to reprogram them in terms of education and retrain them. The education system is important as it relates to young people, because if you talk about good jobs, you've got to talk about good training. You've got to be economically sound yourself and to develop skills so you can become self-supporting.

MR. WOODSON: Several people have expressed concern about why we are spending so much time dealing with something that is obvious to most of you, even though not clearly defined, and why we started with Tee Rodgers and others about what is it that turns young people around.

Let me explain to you. If we're saying that the 4-H clubs and the YMCAs and the other organizations that are receiving the money, that are receiving the recognition, and yet are not effective—it is not enough for me or others to say that, because of the job that these neighborhood groups have done, they are the ones who are the legitimate representatives for young people.

We have to be able to say why neighborhood groups are more effective. What is it that neighborhood groups do that's different from what the Y or other organizations can do for the youths? Those differences are precisely what we're trying to get at here, and it is not enough for adults always to say what's important to young people. I have to be able to say that this is what the young people themselves have said, not their interpreters or translators, but what the young people have said.

What Tee said in answer to the question is important for public policy. Those little things are hard to define. What is it that made a difference in his life? What made him exchange one kind of power base for a different kind of power base, while still maintaining himself within his original group?

A Y can't do that. A 4-H club can't accomplish that. I have to know the other kinds of things. V.G. said that there are many things that are done. You can't do just one thing for all young people, but you do many things for them. The way most other programs are structured, there is a single way of dealing with young people. Young people will be counseled by social workers; young people will report for their treatment every week for one hour. That's the way the system deals with young people now.

If we're saying that what you do is different, then there has to be a public record of that. There has never been a national forum where young people themselves, of the caliber and quality of young people who are sitting around this table, were asked what it is that makes a difference in their lives.

There has to be a public record of it, so that some of us who interpret what you do in the policy community will have evidence for what we believe in our hearts to be true. It's not enough for Bob Woodson to say this; this is my sermon this month, so I'm going up to Capitol Hill and preach that sermon. The congressmen will say, "That's just your opinion. We don't believe you." We have to be able to say that we have called together young people and their sponsors around the country and they have told us this. We're interpreting and trying to analyze what they have said and what they believe. Therefore, this information is not about an isolated case; their comments point this out.

It's the same with the whole issue of enterprise development. None of you wants to be dependent upon the state the rest of your life, to be at the whim of this granting agency, whether LEAA is going to continue to get funds. Most of you don't want to do it. You do it out of necessity. Most of you want to be as independent as any other business person in this society. If you have tee shirts or something that takes off and begins to sell to every tourist who comes through, and millions are marketed around the world, that's income that's going to come into your organization, no matter what your political beliefs are.

Rich people in society have extreme political points of view, both left and right. What makes them independent is they have an independent financial base. They don't depend upon a government grant. That's why it's important. If you believe that you are to try continually to spend your energy gaining more welfare, then you ought to say that. If you believe that you need a more independent base, that you have ideas and energy to devote to enterprise development, then say that. But don't challenge whether the question ought to be raised.

Some of these things are tedious, but you've been invited here maybe to labor with some tedious things, some obvious things that are stupid for people even to ask. I'm asking you stupid questions, then, but I'm asking you to answer these questions. That's the respect I want.

AL MARTIN, the Youth Identity Program: The first grant the Youth Identity Program ever got from the city was from the New York City

Youth Board, for $15,000. That was for 1977–1978. Then for 1978–1979, we got another $15,000. The board called me down there to validate my contract.

I went to the office. Other contracts of other agencies happened to be on the table. Nobody was around, so I tried to see what everybody else got. I looked at this one; this cadet corps got $60,000. I looked at this one; this group got $84,000. Another one got $40,000.

The board tells me what a great job the Youth Identity Program is doing, working in the court system and working in the prison: "You're one of our model programs." I turned around and said, "If we're such a model program, how come we're only getting $15,000 and we are working with kids from all over the city in the prison, and this cadet group is working with probably good kids, and they're getting $60,000–70,000?"

"Well, Al, it's all in politics. You've got to have the right politician backing you." This politician garbage—it's a joke. I went to a politician and asked him to give me a hand getting my grant. From this point on, every time there is an election, he says, "Al, I need your boys. Al, I need your boys." My boys don't want to go out there and vote for this one and vote for that one. Another politician says, "We helped you, also. Can you do this for us?" The politician thing is a joke, but you have to deal with the politicians. That's the thing in dealing in New York City; the city is completely political.

MR. NIZAM FATAH: Another thing happens. I never had a chance to tell Al Martin. But certain officials didn't know that I knew Al. They didn't know our connection from the Bronx and all over town. One guy said, "Don't be mad at me. Be mad at Al Martin." I said, "Al Martin? From where?" He said, "Have you ever heard of the Youth Identity Program in the Bronx?" I said, "Yes, I've heard of it." He said, "He got your money."

I understood the whole thing. I said, "Al happens to be a friend of mine."

The other thing happened with Tommy Hemonds, whom I happen to like. Tommy Hemonds sat in at a roundtable meeting with Flint and me; in fact, at that meeting Flint had been elected chairman of the roundtable board. There were all kind of gangs. Sergeant Hargrove was there. It was the first open meeting when we brought in CBS, and a lot of hot-shots who were supposed to give us some money, and a lot of other people, and let them sit around.

We let Tommy Hemonds sit right there with us. Then, when we went to the youth board, Tommy said, "Your problem still is that we will not fund in New York City, either publicly or privately, anybody who does not advocate the dissolution of youth gangs." An interesting thing was that the pictures that Sergeant Hargrove took of Tommy sitting there with all the youth gangs were blown up, 4 by 8 inches, and hung on his wall to show that the board deals with this type of youth. But we still couldn't get anywhere.

MR. WOODSON: We could spend a lot of time giving our own horror stories about how bad politicians are and about how they rip us off. We should talk about our legitimacy as organizations. We can talk about how bad it is, but let's talk about what are the good things, what are our strengths, what is it that we do that earns for us the right to say, yes, we qualify for funds. That's what we've got to talk about. What influence do we have on young people? What ideas do we have that support what we're saying?

DR. BRIGITTE BERGER: I was on a National Science Foundation grant-giving panel. We had to dish out $10 million in two days. This was for minority institutions, that is, not minority institutions but those with most of their people being minorities. The panel members are not politicians; they are government bureaucrats.

Everything I proposed, the grassroots attempts, was voted down. Everything for hardware, for the stuff that is not needed, was voted in. I was the only one who had a different position. It was not a question of politicians. It's a question of how you write grants, what is the front you are using, how do you use things to your advantage. It's not just who you know, it's much more—on a much deeper level.

MR. DAVID FATTAH: A critical question was laid on the floor that hadn't been addressed; that question is, should we approach the economic system, like your large corporate structures, or should we approach the political system in terms of economics for the benefit of the community?

That's critical, because that is a national question, and that's what's happening to us now. We're able to see that business has won in terms of influencing the government. The government decided to go against inflation at the expense of putting anybody out of work, and it told everybody, "Just hang on until we get the prices down—because it don't matter if you don't have any money anyway—because we've got to make sure that business is all right. If business is all right, then you're going to be all right."

I think it's important that we ourselves are able to leave here feeling that we have gained something. We are constantly giving up at this point. Peter Berger was asking why don't we do this, why don't we do that? A good example of why it is necessary to put the political system in line or take it over by voting, is what happened with us with the numbers.

Every group in this country that has made it, that has been able to survive, has had some kind of economic base it has been able to build on and therefore get out of the kind of problems that we have. Many of the problems that a lot of the youths have, that we have, are there because we don't have money. A lot of times when you can spend that extra hour talking to a youth, showing that youth that your position is correct, it can be completely undercut, because the only person he sees with some money is somebody who is pushing heroin. That has an overriding influence.

When we had the numbers—which was illegal at one time—somebody found that numbers was employing people, numbers was making a lot of money, numbers was giving people Cadillacs, numbers was getting people good jobs. First, an illegal group stepped in to take over the numbers. Then the government looked at it and said, "Numbers is making a lot of money, numbers is employing a lot of people." So the government took over the numbers. Even now, if you're caught writing numbers, you're locked up. But the government tells you every day to take a chance and buy lottery tickets and makes this available to you. That is in effect destroying an industry.

When the government wanted to go to the moon, the government created the aerospace industry and spent all kinds of money so somebody could bring back a moon rock to see if it would walk and talk. That was taxpayers' money. Nothing was said. When these people who were enticed into that industry by salaries from $30,000 up lost their jobs, the government gave them special courses and told them that everything was going to be all right: "Don't panic, don't jump off the bridge." It found a way to employ these people. But when the numbers industry was destroyed, no notice was taken. This is why, out of necessity, pressure should constantly be put on the political system to put our people back to work.

Most people here have put in ten years or more. It's like when the Bible says that a day or a year to God is a long time. When you have spent a month in one of these communities dealing with a gang, that's like ten years of being in a corporation trying to make some money, not just to mention that your life is on the line constantly. You have been hassled constantly. Half of the people in the neighborhood think you're crazy. Just the attempt to do something, let alone the success of being able to get maybe one guy to lighten up, is something.

There are people here who obviously have been struggling, knocking themselves out and hitting their heads against the wall; they get

$15,000, $35,000. We haven't addressed that. We're doing this for love, but whoever is here from a foundation or whatever else should reciprocate. Each of these groups should be able to get some benefit. If somebody needs proposal help before he leaves this conference, somebody should show him how to do it.

Each group sitting here has proved it has the right to be funded. There are other groups that are funded time and time again, like a broken-down car. You keep putting gas in it; it doesn't run, so you buy more gas.

I was talking to some folks here that I haven't met in three years. If we are to save America, people like ourselves have to be found and encouraged and kept moving.

You cannot say to me not to see the government. I've seen the government bring somebody here from over in Korea, somewhere that they told my father to shoot people on sight. He's put in my neighborhood, and his store is stocked. If nobody goes in there, it still runs. Don't tell me not to go see the government.

There are some basic, underlying, hard, cold-blooded issues that need to be dealt with, and before the people leave here, there should be something done to encourage and inspire or perhaps help them to continue.

MR. WOODSON: Everybody has his role. That may be in helping somebody fill out an application or in doing some concrete things of immediate benefit to you here.

The concerns that I have are for those not here. What I do best and what this institute can do best are the things that do not have immediate payoff, but they do have delayed payoffs. As a person who comes from an action orientation, I'm used to running programs and putting money in the hands of people, walking in communities and helping people. To sit down for three years and write a book and go around and study seemed soft at first. Then I began to understand—as I began to generate articles, as I began to talk to people, to speak before the Senate, the House, and began to talk about policy people. Press people began to come, and other people. All this has some benefit in the long run. The role and the function of this conference have to be clear. This conference is not to give you immediate payoffs other than a trip to Washington and an opportunity to sit and learn from one another and share. That seems mighty soft, but that's all that this conference has to offer you. I would be lying if I told you that you're going to leave here with a commitment to get funds next week. Even the foundation people are here at our request—or in some cases, at theirs. This is a conference that AEI put together.

121

I don't want to mislead anybody. You are not here so you can leave and say this is what we took home from Washington, except maybe some rest, some food, some fellowship, some exchange, some new insights and new information, some new contacts that can be the basis of a national network.

The purpose of this conference is to benefit you. If your story, if what you're doing, is analyzed, written about, and published, that way, it begins to penetrate the policy apparatus, and what you believe and what you think has to be dealt with by those who make the kind of decisions that Brigitte Berger talked about. You need a volume of knowledge that supports what she was saying, so that she can say that this is why these groups ought to be getting the money, because a number of business people say it makes sense. More and more people have to begin to understand what you are about.

More people have to be helped. We could have had five times the number of groups invited to this conference, but we kept it small. It is important in this first conference for us to put on the public record and into publication what it is that you are about, so it begins to generate influence.

Already we got press response. Somebody from CBS is going to do a special on one or two of these programs. Sister Fattah and her group were on the radio. There is interest, because the agencies are bankrupt in their approach to dealing with youth crime. They don't know what to do. They have spent $10 million a year in research alone, $449 million in all of these programs. A lot of judges, a lot of prosecutors, a lot of politicians are saying, "We have spent all this money and now when the American public says the dollars are short, we have to cut back, and no solutions have been forthcoming." That means, for the first time, we have to look for answers in other places, and we have to have those answers written down, not just in your heads. We have to have them collectively written down, so people can deal with them.

You have to challenge people on their turf. You don't challenge policy makers while you're back in Los Angeles, because they don't care what happens in Los Angeles. You challenge them on their turf. Their turf is the written word. They don't believe anything unless it's written.

You don't have to do any writing, because I'm going to do that. But, in order for me to do it with any credibility, it can't be Bob Woodson's opinion; policies have to be based upon sound information and a data base. That can only come from you.

MR. NIZAM FATAH: Everybody sends you to these seminars on how you get money, who you ask it from; here is the method, here are the secret fifty ways to get rich. We figured out maybe we could all gang up. All of us could drop one massive proposal and force a foundation or the Justice Department or somebody to recognize us. Maybe we have to have a network decision. Maybe we have to set up a collective, since it is obvious that there is no established modality. There is a methodology, but perhaps we need to put our position together, in a publishable sense. We could set up a replicable program throughout the country, from various organizations and cities with proven success or a track record, veterans of this particular initiative, as it will probably be called at some point. Through this particular initiative, we could set up a network of eight or ten cities to show "how we dealt with it." There must be some certain factors that can be identified which are—as said before—universal to all of our programs that make us successful.

Getting the right response is a problem when we start quoting the statistics of the crime rate, what it costs people in property, human life, misery, not even speaking of the people who are considered the perpetrators of these crimes, but only about the victims. Sometimes response depends on how you say it. Sometimes people don't care about the perpetrator. You might have to show what the victimization is nationally, exactly what we deal with. This is the replication aspect. We are trying to set up a modality to deal with the crime situation whether you are in Germany or whether you are in Dubuque. From this cross section of the United States represented here, maybe we can put together something that the federal agencies might at least try.

It seems they like study programs more than any other type of application. Maybe we could do that here. Maybe that could give us some sort of hope to keep hanging on—to go back and tell our people we might get a study done. Right now, everybody is feeling low.

SISTER FATTAH: What we need and what you need are not mutually exclusive. We can do both. What we need is a communications system. What we need is an economic base. What we need is some political clout.

I can envision, from this group here, selecting the next president. Because if we put all of our youth together, constructively working together, coming up with an agenda, and with the influence we have with youth across the country, that vote that has not been reckoned with, gives us some clout. We will give you what you need: that is, information about us; then we need to sit down and come up with some of the things we need.

MR. WOODSON: We can split the remaining time between your needs and the conference agenda. You can meet and discuss what you need to talk about. That's a beginning. The last time we got together, three years ago, there was just about a quarter of the number of people. That was on a shoestring, a little ragtag meeting. But it was very, very important then. I'm also concerned now about giving the young people a chance to speak.

MR. GUINSES: I've learned a lot from young people, and they may have better ideas than all of us. If we come together, let them be relaxed.

I've failed to identify at least three positive things that we have done in Los Angeles that brought in money. Mr. Fattah brought up a good point: we may not be able to deal with it today, but it may be a thing in the future—maybe next week—to give hope to people, the grassroots people who are trying to do something out there, who are doing it. I'm not concerned about everybody else out there, because they're not concerned about me when I'm involved in a crisis in the community. I'm concerned about the people here. You don't need big heads here, on ego trips, to do something constructive.

The conference, overall, is a constructive thing for me, because I have a chance to meet a lot of people, I've gotten lots of input, and I'm thinking about a nationwide network that could be utilized immediately, as we leave here this week. But I would like to see more input come from the young people as well as from the communities they represent.

SISTER M. ISOLINA FERRÉ, Dispensario San Antonio: Maybe I'm not a young person, but I'm a leader of them. Talking about Puerto Rico, we don't have gangs. When we hear all that's going on in the United States, maybe a gang is a united force. It is also good to know, however, for our people who are coming up here and who you're going to meet, that a gang is a special thing that is not down there. People don't get united. Poor people don't unite. They don't know yet how to unite—neither the economically poor nor the educationally poor. It's a hard thing to do, you know.

We don't have boy scouts or girl scouts or things like that, because they are middle class or upper class. But the poor don't unite. They don't have structures. In our center, we have been trying to educate them to see how together we can do things. Many of our Puerto Ricans are coming up here. Of course, they are joining when they come up here. But down there, they don't have the idea of a united front to do all the things. That's why sometimes they're often phased out. We're marginal in a lot of things.

MR. NIZAM FATAH: The conference has served a lot of purposes for me, because I like the idea of the economic development, especially with Carl Hardrick. I was talking to him about purchasing some tee shirts for his community day, because those things sell. They not only sell to tourists, they sell anywhere. Everybody who is out there working on that particular struggle has pretty much paid his dues, or he wouldn't be here. We have a sense of spiritualness.

MR. HARDRICK: Even though I haven't visited Philadelphia or seen the House of Umoja, I constantly thought about it almost every day, how it was doing. The things that it was doing, I was doing every day. I kept saying, "I've got to get to Philly, I've got to get to Philly."

Sometimes we don't like to hear things. When I started dealing with the corporate structure, I began to hear things that I did not like. But I had to—move to another level. I had to move from the level of seeing that I've got problems, to how will I solve the major problems in terms of economics.

Dealing with the corporate structure is a completely different picture in terms of the tone, the mannerism, the kind of interest that corporations have, given their strictly business interest and their not being in tune with what you are. Yet you have to sell them the very things you are about and what you're trying to do.

I understand where people are coming from when they say it's not in their interest; but it is, at some point. It is, because someone else will ask you these very questions when you go to a funding source. You should be able to know or at least understand that you can contact Dr. So-and-so. I'm going to an insurance company, for instance, and I'd like to know what questions I should be raising, or what should I be about. Who you're dealing with sometimes changes your philosophy—not that you're compromising—but you've got to understand the people, the tactics, to get the things that you want.

When we were dealing with Consolidated, I didn't like dealing with the firm, but I was dealing with it for jobs. The more we talked, the more we communicated. Based on that we were talking with a government agency about fifty units of housing. We found out getting the housing—and this was through young people—turned around jobs. We had to get sanctions from Consolidated to sign off on that proposal to get the fifty units of housing, so we have fifty units of housing based on the tobacco jobs. We didn't have any idea that we had to go back to Consolidated to sign off on the housing. It wasn't interested in housing, but the firm was interested in the work that we were doing with young people. It wasn't interested in dealing with the federal government, but the firm said, "If it's good for the community, and we know that you're doing a good job, we'll sign off on it."

TOMMIE LEE JONES, Youth in Action: Nonprofit, community-based organizations should collectively, across the nation, join a network, whereby we can control our votes. The Ching-A-Lings have over 8,000 members. These members have families—uncles, aunts, and cousins— and friends. Youth in Action has 900 families right now that we're working with, and each family has from eight to ten kids, or cousins and uncles. We have enough people collectively to control the political vote that we need.

We have to work on it. We should leave here today and have Bob Woodson bring us back at some other time and start working on a plan, how we can link a network across the nation. Then the president or the Congress will say to us, "Which way are the community people going to vote, the poor people?" We represent poor people. We cannot fight the government if we have nothing to fight with.

I was the chairman of the NAACP voter registration drive last year. We registered 2,700 people. They had never heard of Tommie Jones before. That's the only time they wanted to know who he is. They didn't know I am a woman. The last day, I went into the office to let them know who I was and that I was tired of trying to beat their system playing my own game. You have to beat the system playing at their game, the way they play it. They need votes; then we'll have our control. President Carter wants to know where's the black vote, how are we going to vote as black people, a body of people. Next year, they will want to know how the community-based organization people are going to vote, the nonprofit groups and the people they are working with.

MS. NIDIFFER: Our director and I testified at a Senate hearing on juvenile gangs in Los Angeles. It's scary what they're talking about doing. They were talking about locking up children eight and nine years old. They proposed $120 million in the budget in California for more prisons. They are saying our kids are all animals and they need to lock them all up.

Last night I had dinner with a lady from the National Council of La Raza here in Washington. She told me that they were trying to take food stamps away from the people. And in defense, there's a missile that's going to cost $2 billion that people want to build. La Raza went against this; the people got things together and had a picture of people using a gun to get baby food, saying, "Are you going to be responsible for this?"

It's scary to think about the decisions officials are making. They want to put more money into research. They ask what the programs have been doing. What has research been doing? They've been researching for years and years and years, and I think that they're just finding new ways to keep us suppressed. They allocate money from up here, and by the time it gets to the street, there's hardly anything. They toss it out to people and say fight over it. That's a way of keeping us fighting among ourselves.

We belong to a coalition, the Southern California Community Crime Prevention Coalition. It's multicultural; there are browns and yellows and whites and blacks and handicapped people. We are uniting together for a common cause. Here we've been talking about getting together and applying for money; the coalition has done that. Nothing may come of it. It scares the system and the bureaucrats and the politicians when people of different colors start uniting, because they've kept us battling each other for so long.

I saw a movie about that not too long ago. People started extending themselves to their neighbors and found that their neighbors weren't so bad and that they had problems. Everybody was helping each other. All of a sudden, you see flashes of the government: "What are we going to do? People are going off of welfare." You see the law enforcement: "What are we going to do? People aren't committing crimes anymore." The whole government was in a panic, because people were getting along. They were helping each other and they were providing jobs. Some people were saying, "I can make room for you." They were giving somebody a job because he needed it.

It is scary. I went to see the community relations person in our area. He said, "We want to work with the community people, and we want to clean up the neighborhood and stop crime." I said, "What scares me is that you guys say this, but do you mean it? What are you going to do if we clean up the neighborhood? You're the number one crime area. You're getting all the money. They're going to take your funds away from you police officers, if we start cleaning up the streets." Maybe that's why the money is going to the wrong people, because they know that those people aren't going to be able to reach the ones who are doing the crimes. It's hard to redo programs when you don't have any funds.

You have a few people who are doing everything. Our director and I, we're both single parents with children. She has one child, I have two. My kids say, "Mom, I never get to see you." What do you do? You have your own children whom you have to spend some time with, but yet you have to do so much to make things better, because these youths are our leaders of tomorrow. You have to do something for them. That's the hope for the future.

MR. WOODSON: Earlier we talked about changing the agenda to give the group a chance to deal with some things people want to deal with. There aren't many opportunities where people can come together like this.

By way of information, I need some brief answers from people around the table as to the two most pressing needs of your organization and the needs of the people you serve. I want to tell you what the federal government has done in juvenile justice and delinquency prevention policies and practices and what is planned for the next three years, to get your response to it, whether it's helpful to what you're doing. The question is, What are the most pressing needs of your organization?

RESPONSES: Funding and education. . . . Education in the sense of training. . . . Training for getting an education to fit in. . . . Jobs and training money, for education. . . . Funding, because without that you can't do much, and community—you know, activities throughout the communities where the people live.

MR. HARDRICK: We need funding, jobs, education, and the ability to make the contacts that are needed; also the ability to sustain good people within an organization, so it can be viable.

MR. MARTIN: Although we received a sizable grant to do our project at Rikers Island, we have no money to operate our base. We're three months behind on rent. We need general operating expenses. The grants are great to do a project like my Rikers project, but there is not a penny of that money going into the operation of the base station. Yet people expect us to produce.

Second, we need more money for jobs. We have a training comnent, but we don't have enough money for a job fund. We have the trainers and we have the young people who want to be trained, but we need money for jobs.

MR. WOODSON: We're talking about the needs of the organization. I know people need jobs, but what do you need to sustain your organization?

RESPONSES: Money programs. . . . When we have work, we still need more money. . . . What we need is jobs; that's what we need, more work. . . . More work, that's right.

SISTER FATTAH: We need the boys' town and technical assistance for the development of the businesses that we want to start.

MR. DAVID FATTAH: Everybody needs the same thing. We need to be able to continue so that these programs can meet their potential, whatever resources that takes.

MR. RODGERS: We have a training program, but we need a bigger training program so we can train the youths in our community. The other thing is nationwide: jobs.

MRS. JONES: We need money, but free money, foundation money, money that doesn't have so many strings attached. We also need more information about different funding that's available. We also should find some way to get the nonprofit, community-based organizations to meet together once a year.

MR. WOODSON: Are you all confronted with many rules and regulations from government agencies that are associated with these funds, that interfere with what you do? What kind of experiences have you had? What kinds of rules and regulations or standards that you have to comply with do you find are difficult or interfere with you?

SGT. HARGROVE: I see one problem. We are required to hire professionals who are acceptable to the funding agency, but not acceptable to the program.

SISTER FATTAH: Because we have a residential program, a group home, we have to deal with a license every year. Before we were discovered, we were doing the same job, without a license. In order to have a license, we have to pass the different standards. The kitchen has to be just so, for the health department inspection. We have to have credentials in terms of the staff; we have to have a professional social worker. We have to have the records kept in such a way. We never kept a lot of records. We didn't think that everybody needed to know everything; some things should be confidential. The reporting responsibilities are a problem. What they ask for—they don't give you enough money to comply with. They tell you your house has to be fixed up but don't give you any money to fix it up. This is ridiculous. It's a bureaucratic nightmare, which is why we want to develop businesses. If you develop those businesses, then you're entitled, in your own home, to have whatever company you want. If it's our house and we decide we want to have eight kids as our company, that's our business.

MRS. JONES: The federal government or the state should give money to the counties and stipulate that some of these funds can be spent by nonprofit community groups. They don't say that now; they don't have

129

to give you this money. You have to get down and start politicking with the county in order to get this money. If they intend a community-based organization to have some money, they should stipulate how much and what kind of group and have some protection, so that we can get the money without so hard a fight.

There's a certain kind of home that the county likes for kids coming out of jail. You have to be married, with children out of the home. You have to have at least two or three bedrooms vacant, so you can have one person sleep in a bed. We can survive with everyone sleeping in the house as long as you have a place to lay your head down. But the county doesn't see that kind of surviving.

The requirements that they put on most homes for temporary shelter are ridiculous. The bed has to be a certain size. You have to have mirrors on the wall and you have to have bureau drawers, things like that. The county wants to know what kind of food you eat. Do you have a nutritional diet, a balanced diet, rather than do you have food in your house? The county wanted written menus. You should deal with life more realistically.

Another example is the CETA program. We have a lot of brothers and sisters who have trouble signing their names and filling out forms. You have to average a certain score before you can be in the program. That cuts out a lot of people who are disadvantaged. You take English and math tests. If you don't get at least a seventy-five or something like that, you're not qualified for the program.

This is for any kind of jobs, sweeping, whatever. Everybody has to take this test. If you don't pass the test, you don't work. These are apprenticeship training programs.

The other thing is, if you're going to serve in some of these programs, you have to be a criminal. You can't be just a poor kid who needs the service; you have to go and break a window in order to be eligible for some of these programs.

MR. HARDRICK: One of the problems we had with CETA, which is run through the youth program for the summer, is the application—five pages thick. It came from the Employment Training Administration (ETA). It was a fact sheet and not an application. ETA puts that out to the youngster to apply for summer jobs. It put out 10,000 of them; of 10,000, 7,000 were incomplete, or the rest of the youngsters didn't even bother to fill them out.

The quota in Hartford was 2,700 jobs to be filled for the summer. When I left yesterday, not even 200 of them were completed. Whoever designed the application, designed it so that kids would not apply. When we sat down with the administrators of ETA, they said that the applications were that way because they wanted more information and they wanted more people to apply for the jobs. You have this problem, if you're not in on the decision making when it comes to information flowing to young people, how to design the application, how do you get the information that you want? If you're not on those particular boards where they make those decisions, then the application screens out more youngsters than it screens in.

MR. GUINSES: In Los Angeles, we're having the same problem with the summer jobs. They are requiring everybody to bring in proof of age, address, name, status. The main office will be interviewing everybody, instead of the centers. Before, we used to interview the kids and we knew which kids were going to work for that summer.

MR. DAVID FATTAH: Summer jobs—it's just a game they play with us. They give us 100 jobs, and just my community alone has 70,000 people. I know 10,000 of them are disadvantaged youths. We've got to stop taking those summer jobs, because they don't do anything. When we had gang problems, the jobs created more problems. They give you 100 jobs for a city that big. We've got to stop taking this stuff from them.

MR. GUINSES: We used our summer jobs to benefit ourselves. We have work sites where we place our kids.

MR. DAVID FATTAH: We do the same thing, but we don't even need that.

MR. GUINSES: We work with about eight different gangs in our area. We pick one guy from each gang and we place them in the same place.

MR. DAVID FATTAH: We do the same thing.

MR. GUINSES: They have to work many weeks together.

MR. ALLEN: They give Philadelphia 100 jobs. We have 10,000 kids who need jobs where I live. What are you going to do, drop 100 in there, with 9,900 left back? Taking 100 just creates more problems, because all summer long you have to hear that, "She got a job four years in a row. We aren't getting any."

MRS. JONES: Yes, that's right. This is like saying, "Here, you have this many jobs; quit bothering us."

MR. ALLEN: That's it. Now we can't even pick our own people; we have to pick who they say.

LEWIS FIELDS, Youth in Action: Some of the trouble you might have with applications, as far as young people are concerned, comes from trickery. You might have 600 slots. At the same time, the individual has to go for an interview, then a second interview. He would have to go by himself. That made it hectic about three years ago. The kids had communications problems with the office, and they didn't want to go through the drudgery of filling out a lot of different papers.

This is how our agency came into effect as far as job career development is concerned. Mrs. Jones wrote a job description saying that we needed a job career development counselor, and we received that slot. All that counselor did that summer was go to the houses, pick up the kids, and take the kids to both of the interviews. That resulted in moving from having 100 of the 500 slots available three years ago, to 350 slots available. We try to curve with the system. At the same time, no one tells you about a youth advisory board and having someone from your organization join the board because we are affiliated with more youths than anyone in the community. No one lets you know that before those decisions are made for the two interviews and for so many applications. We found out these things after the board was established.

MR. DAVID FATTAH: I found a couple of flagrant things. The government tells us that CETA is the main tool to fight unemployment, but the people don't have any input in CETA. It's not aimed at the urban situation per se. The people in the rural areas take it and run wild with it. As a result of a lot of things that they're doing there, like when we had our program first started, they would change regulations in the middle of the program, which would naturally find you out of compliance. Many times this was done without people having an opportunity to know that there could be a hearing or anything. The formula that they have for CETA is not geared to help the places that have the most unemployment; it's geared to a lot of other things.

The other problem occurred at least at one time in Philadelphia. If you had some ambition, you could go down to the waterfront and get yourself some fruit and set up a vending stand. A lot of brothers who couldn't get jobs, for whatever reasons, were selling cultural artifacts and setting up these vending stands. The city council passed a law that there had to be so many feet between vending stands; you had to have 50-inch wheels on them. Other rules were wiping people off the sidewalk. Yet, when that rule was enforced, the police didn't go down to Ninth and Washington Avenue, where people have been vending for years. They didn't do anything with the Orientals; they've got a little wheel, about 3 inches, but nothing was said.

These are the kinds of things that make people react. In fact, there was a lot of confusion around what the city council did, because those brothers who couldn't get jobs were lost. Philadelphia has lost a great deal of federal money because the CETA program was so mismanaged. They're constantly dealing with the administration. We lost 5,000 jobs in one year, and the administration hardly said a word about it.

Do they want to punish us, first of all, because of what somebody like Mayor Rizzo says to President Carter? Of course, when President Carter came to town, Mayor Rizzo wouldn't sit with him in the middle of Chestnut Street—okay, that cost us about $40 million in grants. The other thing is, when the money does come there, the dude can be mismanaging it. It's like our housing program in Philadelphia; it's all political patronage. You have a bunch of committee people working there who may not show up for work.

As a result, two things happen. One, people who could use a job don't get one, because a lot of these dudes have two jobs; they are retired and hired back. The other thing that happens is that the housing program in Philadelphia is in shambles. These are some problems that can be eliminated if the federal government would deal with the community.

MRS. JONES: Under CETA, the most an average person can make is $10,000. In administration, they can make far more than that. You can only hire one person in a family through the CETA workers, but in Delaware County the CETA administration is all run by a family—cousins, uncles, and aunts. Through CETA, if there are eight in the house, they're making $2,000 a year. It doesn't give you much to work with.

Then they have these young white boys seventeen to eighteen years old come down to Chester and fire kids on our job. We had to fight last year to get some kids reinstated, because one of these boys came down and he didn't like what they were saying; he fired them. I wasn't there; Lewis wasn't there. When we came back, I told them, "Okay, you go and bring in NAACP." As soon as I mentioned that, the officials came down and apologized, "We're sorry, they are not fired, he made a mistake." These are the kinds of things that go on.

PATRICIA FOUNTAIN, Youth in Action: As a result, if you went to the prime sponsor's office of a CETA program—this one is outside Chester—last year and the year before, you might have no minorities or one minority in the whole administrative package. When the kids came for

133

their personal interviews at the CETA main office, they were not interviewed by someone that can relate to their cultural ties and understand that they need the jobs. They were interviewed by someone out of their culture, just out of school. They are looking for specific answers. In the interview, you have to say specific things.

Those kids did not respond that particular way, because they didn't have any training. Because they didn't respond, they did not get the job. As a result, we contacted the office; we told the administrators about the situation. This year they have five minorities doing interviewing in the prime sponsor center. They could have done that five years ago.

MR. WOODSON: When I attended a community meeting in Mrs. Jones's neighborhood, city officials showed me pictures of a recreation center, a house that was converted and a program established without your knowledge.

MRS. JONES: A lot of tricks are played on you, a lot of things are done, just to irritate you. They opened the center and they got everything started, the exact same thing that we were doing. Yet we were told that we could not do it; it was out of our range.

That's not the only time that happened. We went to the prime sponsor and said that we would like to be the agency that would do the interviewing in the city, because we knew the families. We knew all the families almost by first name; we knew something about just about everybody in Chester and what their needs are. We know the kids who don't need jobs; we know the ones that need jobs. They told us that no way could that happen, that it would have to come through the employment agency.

Two months later, they had made an announcement that the prime sponsor at the Media office was going to do all the interviewing. That means that our kids had to go from Chester to Media, in order to be interviewed for the jobs that were available in our city—with no public transportation.

MR. FIELDS: A little time after that, there was the organization that was duplicating the same kind of services. The officials told us that we couldn't do the interviewing. Three months later, they said, "We're going to start doing group interviews at this particular center in Chester." They paid a person to do the interviewing in their office from CETA. This is the same thing that we had explained to them maybe a year, a year and a half, ago.

There was a national organization called Child Care. At one time, the Child Care branch in Chester was dealing with a specific age bracket and did not deal with all the youths of the family. We're talking about fourteen to eighteen. We had talked to Child Care about Youth in Action and how we deal mainly with the youths of a particular age and then we go on with the family.

Child Care was referring these youths with family problems to Youth in Action. Two years passed; Child Care became Children and Youth Services of Delaware County. All that had to be done was to fund us for the youth part and keep Child Care for its part. But the county didn't do that. Children and Youth Service, under the Youth Service part, has four components with about thirty staff people. This is discouraging, when we only have two people or three people and our caseload is almost 400. In fact, that agency is still referring kids to us.

MRS. JONES: Those kids that they are working with come to our agency to complain, "Delaware County Children and Youth Service cannot serve me, but we need your service." Yet we don't have the staff or the means or the resources to work with them.

SISTER FATTAH: We have to look at it from the top in terms of CETA. When CETA administrators wanted to slice the budget, they sliced the youth jobs. If they would fund the community-based organizations directly from Washington, they would cut out ten times the money. The community-based organizations—I'm not talking about the Urban League, I'm talking about community-based organizations—have more integrity in terms of dealing and knowing from the grassroots level which youth is actually going to report to work and stay on a job and which youth is shucking and jiving and just taking up people's time and energy. They cut out LEAA and the community anticrime program, which was doing just that, the same way. They take the money and put it into research.

This is why you have to develop a mechanism to deal with those people who make the decisions. Even if anybody believed the budget was going to be balanced, there's a way to do it, so that you're not hurting the people: cut the fat out of administration.

MR. NIZAM FATAH: In New York, I've been opposed to the summer youth program, that CETA thing. For a long time, I've been vocal about it in the newspapers and everything; that, of course, has also maybe not helped us to be as popular as we would like.

With our particular program, we depend on 90 percent volunteer services from our particular youths. They come in every day, bursting to do everything. This is what the organization is supposed to be about.

Then, when they get those CETA jobs, the way it's set up in New York, you can't pick any youths at all; it's a lottery system. They'll send us a bunch of kids whom we don't know, have never seen; my guys are still there without being paid. Here comes a bunch of kids who have no idea about the organization. They're only here for six weeks anyway. There is nothing you can teach anybody in six weeks; in fact, we don't even try any more.

We did try—we took it for two years, in fact. Flint ran the program. We took them for two summers. It hurt my heart to become involved in that. But I said maybe I'm wrong, because maybe some little black or Puerto Rican kid might want to try and so I'll try it.

We brought the kids in. In the first place, Flint and I almost had to beat them up and throw them out; they didn't know what we were about. What can we teach anybody in six weeks? They're only here a few hours a day. The whole thing is such a haphazard type of programming. About the only thing we can let them know about a job is that you've got to get here on time and stay until it's time to leave. That's important; a lot of people don't know getting to work is important. Once you get there, maybe you can figure out something to do.

Repeating what Sister Falaka was saying, had it not been for a discretionary area where I was able to deal directly with the Office of Juvenile Justice so that the money was coming directly to us, the grant would have gone through Mayor Koch or some of the hot-shot politicians in New York. We would have been totally shut out.

The only way I can—in fact, the only way that any of us can—get any help, especially from the federal government, is for the money to come directly to the organizations. This would eliminate the political considerations, except where you always need a connection here and there. You wouldn't have to do lobbying in order to get your money. All you would have to do is be able to show community interaction, that you have credibility in the community with other community agencies and functions.

MRS. JONES: You wouldn't have to sell your soul; that's what you have to do now to get the money. They make you beg. We've been trying to get money from Children and Youth Services for two years. It's been giving me bits and pieces of information that I need, in order to make everything right to be eligible for this money.

The first time I submitted a proposal, I was told, "We don't have any money." I didn't take no for an answer. I said, "Okay, then I'm going to resubmit it." I did that. A year later, I was told, "You have to have a license." I said, "Why didn't you tell me that last year, so I could have worked toward getting a license?" After we got that information, in another six months I was told I had to be approved by labor and industry.

By this time, we had been evicted from our building. We could have passed inspection. We had moved to a school building, which no one would have approved in the condition it was in. Six months later, I had to take a group of people to the county commission, playing politics—the committeemen and some committee people and the NAACP and other people—just to bring a front of people. They told me everything that I need to know, all at once.

Then I got a call saying, "Would you like to do an employment program? Maybe there's some money for employment." It will be another two years, if I take it like that. You see, they keep you hanging on, they squeeze you.

MR. HARDRICK: With summer jobs, in Hartford you sometimes are a lot closer to the decisions that are being made, or at least you are sitting at the table when a lot of decisions are made that affect you. With the summer jobs, we put in a proposal for $25,000 for a total youth proposal; that deals with equipment, supervisors, in-kind services, training, and so forth. We designed in the training program what we thought young people need and who should do the training. CETA disagreed in terms of the potential of the trainers. CETA thought they should have master's degrees and Ph.D.'s; we thought that people should come from the prison system, the community, and so forth.

We won the battle anyway because we fought in terms of what we thought young people need. We had tied the overall plan into the private sector. We would take a hundred youngsters through a seven-week program. After seven weeks, those young people would automatically move into the insurance program. CETA saw the credibility of the agency tying into a corporate structure; so it was willing to lend some flexibility, because that office wasn't able to do it.

Sometimes you can take soft money and make it work, but you have to have a well-planned program so the sponsors can buy into it. It has to be planned, scheduled, day by day, hour by hour—what that young person is going to be doing from the time that program starts, from July 7 to August 27, in terms of where he is going to be at every given time.

The main thing that we were concerned about was exposing young people to jobs, exposing them to the type of jobs, the type of careers that they should be into, so that when they do make that decision, they can make the best decision, given the best information.

MR. GUINSES: With these summer programs, there are special federal guidelines that state what the issues are—and we got it for the past five years. I'll only take preselected youngsters from the community. I will not allow any youngster to come from the outside to our ground. You can preselect if you make them show you the federal guideline, but it's a special request from the agency. Especially if you're dealing with the type of youngster we are dealing with, they must take into account anything that is endangering your youngster's life. A guy coming into the wrong neighborhood because of some kind of work is either going to get his behind kicked or he's going to pay protection out of his paycheck. If he thinks he's bad, he's going to fight the whole neighborhood; that's endangering your whole agency.

That type of guideline has cleared us for five years; we've got 125 youngsters preselected. But you have to demand that. Other agencies that were with us refused to take the youngsters, too, on those same conditions, so they have to come through and issue it out to you. But it took an agency to go about it on that basis, because that's what you're doing, you're endangering a youngster's life.

MR. NIZAM FATAH: In New York, the entire Catholic diocese stopped taking any of the kids for that same reason. It didn't make any difference, because the way the city government is handling the CETA funds there, they are going to municipal agencies to decide on distribution.

Here's how they claimed I was going to get my kids. They said, "We're going to give it to legal aid or we're going to give it to the police department, and the police department will try to get guys that you might want. Okay?" After the youths came, I said, "What about you? What kind of person are you?" One of the kids said, "I had two homicides and I had so and so." They sent all these nuts to us, and we can't even get our own kids summer jobs.

Then we said, "Let us be the project sponsor." There was too much money involved in that for us—which was just peanuts—so they wouldn't do that. But they wanted us to have these kids come into our office, and nobody was getting paid from it. Flint, did you get anything out of it? Nothing came out of that particular project. We had to pay for that out of our pocket, just to keep this kind of kid going. It's an impossible situation with Mayor Koch in New York. We gave it up totally. This year, we refused to accept summer jobs. We wouldn't even deal with it.

MR. HARDRICK: With the summer program, agencies can do an effective job, given the planning and the technical assistance that they need to put the package together. That's what the federal government does not do. Federal agencies do not give you the technical assistance and the planning time and the money that you need to get the kind of things that you need to be effective. You have to get that from outside; they will tell you that in a minute: "We're not giving you staff people." It's difficult for you to be effective if you don't have the staff people who have the kind of control to run the programs that you know are going to be effective among young people.

MR. NIZAM FATAH: There's another thing that they do, for instance, when it comes down to how they make their selection of project sponsors. Sometimes I'll say, "How did you know about that group?" They say, "We sent an application to this person." When I call up there, I can't even get an application. "We're out of it, we'll get it over there to you in two weeks." It's as if there are preselected agencies. It's not an open competition. It's not a thing that you even know about. Finally, so that they could get themselves off the hook, they did send me an application three days before the deadline. I knew what that was. I just bowed out of that particular area. CETA has a bad taste in New York with most agencies.

SISTER FATTAH: I want to echo what has been said. They will send us, through the lottery system, kids to work at the House of Umoja, when the kids who live at the House of Umoja don't have summer jobs. The only jobs we have for them is to work around the House of Umoja. It's ridiculous. If you don't take it, they say you're not interested in youth employment.

MRS. JOÑES: You would think these programs were designed to keep people fighting and at odds with each other.

MR. HARDRICK: You sometimes have to look at what the program is designed to do and to fight against it to make it work the way you think it should work. That's a difficult thing to do. Given the staff resources that you have, it's difficult. It can be done, but it's a major task for some people to do if they don't have the expertise or the resources or the capability of putting that proposal together.

We refused, for example, to do the lottery system, because other agencies didn't do it. The Hartford Stage had a program where it insisted on hiring its own people. The stage people said they had them at the theater during the winter and they wanted to keep them in the summer. We're saying yes, let them keep their people, and certainly we're going to do the same thing. We selected all ninety of ours.

MR. NIZAM FATAH: The lottery system was to correct a wrong. The wrong was that all of the judges' sons and the politicians' kids were getting the jobs. The city came up with the lottery system, so at least everybody would have an equal shot. But it is not an equal shot, because if you're dealing with a kid whose choice is either to have a job or to go to jail, that's unequal. It's not saying that both of those kids are not capable of doing the job, but the kid who needs the job to stay out of jail should have a preference over the kid who just needs a summer job.

MR. DAVID FATTAH: We fail to realize some things in summer programs. There are two reasons most of us can identify as to why it's a real dilemma. One reason is the *be cool* attitude. We were having a heavy gang thing in Philadelphia. First, people would find out who's who, who's what: "You all going to be cool?" Before then, it was the riot. They'd call everybody in, gather everybody: "You going to be cool?" We'd say, "Okay, we need some gigs." The officials would throw them down. It was like welfare, a check without your being told it was a welfare check.

They would tell me to go out and find the worst folks I could, the real troublemakers, and be sure either they got a job or the gang they were working with got a job. Then the politicians saw that the heat was off when they picked up on the summer jobs. Then you've got committee people going through the neighborhood, giving jobs to people they think are going to keep them in power.

As a result, that matter of the summer job situation has finally been, more or less, transferred into the hands of people like us. We inherited all of these way-out troubles, with the worst one being this: it is a job to decide the difference between some kid going back to school or not going.

If you say, "Hey, man, I'm not going to deal with the summer jobs," then maybe a more corrupt dude will grab them and say, "Look, man, I've got the summer jobs." It became a real power play, because suggestions were made to folks about the summer jobs, which they did not use until they felt it would benefit them. We went to city hall. I asked, "Why don't we get some people, get the young people, let them paint the walls during the summer, and pay them for it?" They said, "They can't paint, they can't draw." We said, "We'll do it like you do number painting. Artists will do the outline, and they'll put the colors in." The guys said, "That's impossible. You can't do it. The union is against it." Two summers later, they did it because it made them look good.

The problem that we have now, if we say no summer jobs—which is the situation they put us in—is that they don't say you can change it. They say either you can have it the way it is or you just don't get it. If we say no summer jobs, then we go back to the young people and we've got a hassle, because they don't understand the aggravation we've been going through. When the summer was over, then it was fun—"Wow, man, we're going to do that next summer"—and you'd be breaking camp.

The other thing was the cash flow. The summer job program gets so that you don't know if you can pay the youth. We'd be sitting there until eight o'clock at night and not know—and you're looking at fifty people who'd been working in the hot sun. They don't look pretty, looking at you real funky, talking about where is the money—and you've got some dude downtown asking you about Form XYZ or, "Let me see if you've got all your paperwork in." Here are these people standing on your porch, looking at you funny. You understand?

By the time you get that hooked up and you get through that summer with them, here they come again. Kids dig the summer program. For some reason, it's one of those romantic things. (When the summer is over, most of us have to work two jobs.)

The city will say, "Okay, you can have some workers and you all can clean the lots." You assume they're going to send you some shovels and brooms if they're talking about cleaning lots, right? But they don't. Then you get all these dudes mad at you: "Man, there ain't nothing to do. Man, this is jive. You all don't have anything to do. I'm going to drink some wine. Look, I'm going to smoke this. When you all get it straightened out, let me know."

Until we get more control over the summer job program, we're going to be more or less forced to deal with it, because we don't have anything else to throw down there. It disrupts your entire program. In the summer, if you're handling a summer youth job program, for everything else you are doing, you might as well just say, "Look, you all, the other stuff is going to be derailed for three months while we try to suffer through this thing."

MR. WOODSON: Everybody is nodding in agreement on that, right?

MR. ALLEN: That's what they want you to do. That's why they're giving us the hassle, that's why they're taking us through so many changes, so that the program would cop out and they'd say forget it. Then there will be no jobs at all. They're only giving us a limited amount anyway. If seven or eight more organizations say they won't take it, where are they going to get it—they're not going to give them all up. They're going to give them to whomever they want to give them to, and the communities then are the ones that lose.

MR. NIZAM FATAH: Speaking about creation of problems, I ran the program for a couple of years for a New York club. When my own children, the gangs I'm affiliated with, came into the center, there wasn't a door locked or a drawer locked. My stationery was there. Last year, I had to beat about three kids over the head with a telephone book; I blew my top. Here were some kids, we're trying to do something for them, and I caught them walking out with all the stationery of ICRY. They had it in their pockets. They had no need for it. It was just to take it. When we used the gangs, in five years—we've had cameras, everything, lying all over the office—we've never had to lock up anything anywhere for any reason. It has always been either the adults we've been dealing with or people who come from the middle class who are problems. The kids have never taken anything, except for these kids who didn't have any commitment to the agency in the first place. They didn't know what we were about.

You can't quit certain functions, but actually it wasn't even in our province to make the decision on summer jobs. It was out of our hands. We weren't getting it anyway. It was too costly for us to continue to try to run this function in New York. We couldn't even be crew chiefs. They wouldn't even pay us as crew chiefs. You can't be a crew chief, so there is no supervision. The crew chiefs came from the legal aid; some were college students.

They are saying that the older generation complained so much about jobs, why should you have to get paid when we're giving you the jobs for your youths?

But other people are being paid for it. These people want you on political campaigns. They are always calling you up to do this or do that for them or, "Why can't you clean up your neighborhood, and why can't you do this kind of thing?" I say, "Sanitation is making $26,000 a year, why can't they do it? Why do we have to police our neighborhoods?" They've got cops making all that kind of money who are being paid to do that, but they are telling us that if we want our neighborhoods clean, we have to volunteer to do this for nothing.

That's a hard thing for me to explain to these youths. I keep telling them, "Hey, look, okay, the system is nothing, but maybe we can circumvent this or circumvent that, see it working." They just want to know why we always have to do the volunteer work, why we never get paid for this kind of thing.

Crazy Cat is not on our payroll in any way. They say, "Hey, interact with other agencies." We've been around to fifteen different places that called, that get these big, million-dollar grants, and then they say, "Look, send the kids over there." They're always hitting on us for referral stuff or sending their people over to us, but apparently we don't have enough credibility to get proper funding, appropriate funding, or even adequate funding. The same agencies that they give the big money to are constantly leaning on us for their credibility. You send people over there when they say, "We have so many jobs." The guy comes back, and I say, "What happened?" The guy says—this will be in February—"They told me to come back in September when they are hiring and put my name down, fill out this thing." They want to see him about five times in the interim, incidentally.

MR. ALLEN: I agree with Brother Fatah. They're not going to give us those jobs for the people in our own community, but they're going to send somebody in there.

First of all, when they give us some jobs, they don't give us enough. Then they're going to send somebody from somewhere else to work there. They're going to pay somebody from somewhere else to come work in our neighborhood there when we can do it and we could have our own people, whom we know, working there. We don't need that.

MR. HARDRICK: Little Brother Rob is right in what he's saying. When you take on CETA, you take on the administration costs. What they are saying to you is, "Here, we want your man-hours, but we are not going to give you the money to cover the things that you need, nor the paper work that has to be done. You have to do that on your own."

If you're going to get on a summer program, you have to buy that and sell that to someone else: "Look, we have a summer program, but we do not have supervisors, we do not have the administrators, and we do not have people to document the kinds of things that we need to document, so that we can continue doing the positive things for young people."

You have to sell the particular summer program that you need for staffing to an agency or to a corporation to buy into, so you can run an effective summer program. CETA expects you to do it for nothing.

MR. MARTIN: I had a summer program two years ago and bowed out the second year. This year I don't want to be bothered with it. So far this year, we've had offers of about 155 jobs from various sponsors that are looking to dump the summer workers off. I told them I can't use them.

First when I talked to them, I said, "Look, we need a certain type young person, a male between eighteen and twenty-one, because the only place I have for them is over on Rikers Island, and I have to select them and then put them through the screening." When I put down those particulars, nobody wanted to deal with me and give me summer jobs. It's a hassle; it's a phony.

MR. RODGERS: With some of the problems that came up, you stated a problem. Except for Rob Allen, I didn't hear the solution. In Los Angeles, when they gave us job slots and sent their "college" counselors over to us, they couldn't handle us. Not physically, they couldn't handle us mentally.

After that, they say, "Hey, this thing is so tough; we don't want to go over there and mess up their program." They didn't want to deal with us, one on one. With the things that we do, with street counseling, they would have to come down and counsel on the streets, and they said, "Oh, no, we just do paper work." That stopped all of that for the college kids coming down there and trying to show us how to run our thing. But I wanted to hear from Rob Allen what happened when they sent the college kids over there.

MR. ALLEN: In Philadelphia's summer program, at one time we could pick who we wanted. If there were any money to pay staff, then we would have our own staff. Now that they have a lottery, you can't do that. They're going to pick whom they want to send to us. They send you different monitors there anyway. Most of the time, when they come in and they catch on to the situation, they just try to stay away until they've got to come and drop off the paychecks.

We should draw up a proposal where they have to give jobs on the basis of the size of the family. If there are four in a family, they should be able to give at least one person in that family a job; if there are twelve, they should be able to give at least four of them a job in each community. That's not too much to ask, because they have the money to do that.

They'll take 10,000 jobs, give us 100 jobs for 17,000 people in the community, and expect us to deal with that. Then they're going to send us 100 more for someone else to come there, where they could have given us that money for the extra 100, and we could have brought 200 more from that community.

Instead of our going through these changes where you've got ten kids and they say there aren't any jobs and these other kids get the jobs, tell them we don't need that. I don't want it. Tell them to keep it. They're going to have to do something, because they're not just going to let the money sit there; they'll have to do something. We have to put some pressure on. We are the ones who put them in office to make these decisions for us; we've got to make them accountable to us.

SISTER FATTAH: The lottery system is the law in Philadelphia. We don't have what V.G. was talking about, any preference. The only people who get preference are the Catholic diocese and the school system. We're not the Catholic diocese, and we're not the school system. We would have to tell those kids who are coming to us that they can't work at the House of Umoja, and we didn't have the heart to say that to them. With our own kids, we had to do as we always have to do; we had to make some hard decisions. We had a long rap session with them. We let the kids make the decision whether we should send those other kids away. Our kids said rather than stand in the way of some other kid having a job, they would let them come. It worked out only because our kids are big enough in their hearts to say they wouldn't stand in somebody else's way. It's wrong to have to put that burden on them. Why do they always have to be the understanding ones? This is why we said we don't want any more. We want to go into business. There is no reason in the world why those tee shirts can't come to Philadelphia, for us to sell the tee shirts and split the profit in New York. There is no reason why the photographs from Puerto Rico can't come to Los Angeles, and we sell them, or Christmas cards, or what have you. We need to go into business, we need to be independent. The time and energy that it takes to rap and talk and explain constantly, how long can we do that? Economic independence, self-determination, means exactly that: that's the direction in which we want to go. We're tired of the game. We are very tired!

MR. HARDRICK: Last summer, I sat on a vice-presidential task force on youth employment that was held at the insurance companies. I went the wrong day.

There was a day for community groups and there was a day for industry. I went when industry was there. The sister told me, "Carl, you're not supposed to be in here, but now that you're here, you might as well take a seat." They had the people from the factories and corporations; everybody was there. I couldn't believe what I was hearing. They were personnel people, presidents of corporations—they were saying there are plenty of jobs for young people.

Tears were running from my eyes. They were saying, "We can't find youths." This is what came out. They made a transcript. Sister Jones was the one who helped put it together; there was somebody from Brandeis University who coordinated it with the youth employment.

I listened to the corporations say that there are plenty of youth jobs and youth employment, not only for the summer but year around—year around—and they tell you, "We're looking for them." Then they got the *but*—"But we can't deal with the attitude they come there with. We

145

had some Puerto Ricans come in and they were too loud. We had to fire some blacks because of the language that they were using."

By the tone in which folks were saying it and the effectivensss that people have with the things that they're doing best, some of that was true and probably some of that was not. I spoke of racism, and then they finally agreed that there was a lot of racism that the young people had to be confronted with, once they came into those companies.

They're probably looking for ways to employ youth, in terms of the employment services which require them to bring young people in, and it's who brings them in there and how they come in that counts. At some point you have to consider if there's soft money, how do you utilize it to set up a program that can be effective, that someone can look into and tie it into some hard-core money?

MR. ALLEN: We went to the city and we told the city that we wanted the brothers from the street to have a contract to deal with abandoned cars. Nobody knew better how to strip cars than the brothers we were dealing with. Rather than have the cars stay there—we wanted the community to be beautiful—the brothers could strip the cars down, take the parts, put them together in some old cars, then sell some of the cars they didn't need.

We thought that made sense. The city said, "Come on, let's talk about it." When we went in to talk about it, the city started talking about, "Who is going to buy out insurance?" There should be insurance on the kids so that they would be allowed to do this. They always have some kind of blockage. No matter how creative or innovative an idea is, there is some kind of blockage that they have, some kind of legal, bureaucratic thing.

SISTER FATTAH: They just don't want you to do it. A year later, we were watching television, and there was this exposé on a friend of Frank Rizzo's who had the contract to go in there and take care of those old cars. We couldn't believe it. They were going to indict him, send him up.

MR. DAVID FATTAH: He had a record as long as your right arm. He'd been giving money; he got caught. They have renewed his contract. When all this came up, the guy just shook his head, "Why do you want to pick on me?"

The main thing is to look at what is happening. There is a conflict in what we are about as opposed to what other people are about. There is a direct conflict there; you can tell. Just like in the army, at war, it takes nine people to support one soldier in the field. That's how they look at these programs; this is not about us getting the cash. They say, "If I give him a job, I've got to be able to hide nine other people to keep them in business," whether that's shuffling papers, whether that's checking on you, whether that's coming through your neighborhood asking your neighbor, "Are you a horse thief?" This is how we keep getting chopped off. We're going to have to take the bull by the horns at some point.

We are going to have to sit down and start calling the shots on these programs that they say are for us, or we're going to have to refuse collectively to participate. If we refuse to participate, across the board, then those other eight people that were hired are going to have to lose their jobs, too.

MR. ALLEN: That's exactly what we were saying earlier. Maybe you can't elect a guy, but you can stop him from being elected.

SISTER FATTAH: Then they can't play it off if all of us stopped at one time. One of the worst things that can happen in the city if people get tired of different things is everybody just doesn't go to work.

MR. NIZAM FATAH: Somebody gave a war and nobody came.

MR. GUINSES: What I'm concerned with is not only stopping, but how you move. How do you move a boys' town? How do you make it work? How do you tie in to the people who can make it work? How do you tie into being self-supporting? How do you get the business technology, the expertise, that you need so you can grow, as well as the brothers?

SISTER FATTAH: If we establish our own communications network and we establish our own economic base, if we, the groups, ourselves, depend on each other—all we have is each other—we can do it. We're not going to jive each other.

We have industries. We know publishing. *Umoja* magazine could come out again, and we could distribute it in every key city, so brothers would have a voice to say what they want to say. We could sell the tee shirts. We could sell jewelry, handmade jewelry, like the brothers who can't vend anymore. There are all kinds of products and things. The technical assistance we need is only from people who are in business; we will be in business, too.

MR. HARDRICK: You're still going to have to build bridges to the other side of the river.

SISTER FATTAH: Nobody here denies that; nobody is opposed to building a bridge. We can look eyeball to eyeball. What has happened in this country is, they don't respect us. If they respected us, then they wouldn't have been arguing this week about food stamps. What they have done is to take away everything that was fought for in the 1960s. They've taken it all away in the 1970s. There is definitely a lack of respect. When you talk about a partnership, a partnership has to be an equal thing where you're sitting with the same power that I am. Then we're partners. Otherwise, there's a big imbalance. You've got to have a base of power of your own, and that's what we're talking about building, so they'd have to listen.

MR. AGOSTO: I remember something Percy Sutton told me. He said, "A lot of minority people think if you put your votes together, you get a political base and you become strong and then you get some money later on. That's impossible and it has never happened in history, it has never happened anywhere." He said that you do not get money after you establish a political base. He said you first get the money and *then* you establish a political base. You must have something to fund yourself in order to make a political move.

We're going to have to start counting our dollars together, in order to establish a political power. In the first place, it is not that minorities, blacks particularly, or Puerto Ricans and Chicanos, are not aware of the political system. It's just that they don't have time or the convenience to become involved in it, because it's an everyday hand-over. It's not that we're so stupid and unsophisticated that we don't know we must become a part of the system, but everybody is too hungry to deal with that.

It's like that even with your wife. Maybe a guy is arguing with his wife, but he doesn't have time. He's got to do this or that: "I'll deal with that later; I'll deal with it." That's the same thing they're doing with the political system: "I'll deal with that later; right now, I've got to eat. How can I deal with this? I've got to deal with this first, then I'll worry about who is going to be the president."

MR. WOODSON: I'd like to mention something about what the federal policy looks like over the next few years. For the past couple of years, I have been looking at what the federal government has been doing through the Office of Juvenile Justice and Delinquency Prevention. That agency was given the lead role by Congress in the whole area of delinquency prevention and juvenile justice. My approach to evaluating or assessing the policies of any organization or government is to look at where it spends its money. While it says that 98 percent of the money has been spent on juvenile justice—$449 million over five years spent by the juvenile justice office—that money has been spent primarily for the deinstitutionalization of status offenders.

Also, programs aimed at diverting youngsters have been funded, again going to the traditional organizations: the YMCAs, the Federation of Boys Clubs, the 4-H Clubs, the Federation of Womens' Clubs, the Federation of Jewish Womens' Clubs, the Red Cross. They have been the recipients of the bulk of these funds.

Of about 390 funded programs, fewer than 30 have gone to minority organizations. Those minority organizations funded have been the National Urban League, the National Association of Darcy Heights, the National Council of Negro Women—few grassroots organizations.

To give you an example of how diversion money has been spent, a lot of it has gone to police departments and other programs like that. The transit police in New York City received a $500,000 grant to divert youngsters from the juvenile justice system. They were arresting youngsters at the turnstiles and "counseling them and diverting them." They found that the number of youngsters eligible to be diverted sharply declined; there just weren't many kids available. They were in danger of losing the $500,000. They took some youngsters who were jumping the turnstiles—which is a summary offense—and charged them with delinquency, so that they would then be eligible to be diverted from the system. That meant that the youngsters had a record, and then the personnel policies of the New York City Transit Authority police changed to equate a juvenile arrest with a felony arrest, as a condition for promotion.

I found out, through the National Black Police Association, that this is true in Chicago and in other cities throughout the country. There is a trend that has not been verified through any research, but through the comments of minority police officers throughout the country. Personnel practices in police departments are going to have more to do with increases in crime—at least reporting increases in crime—than anything the kids are doing. Some of the kids in those urban centers are going to be classified as delinquent, as a condition for these people getting this diversion money.

Not only are these programs not helping, but, in many instances, they are making the situation much worse. Almost every state in the union has on its books a law that is similar to the ones in New York, California, and Illinois. Youngsters thirteen years old can be remanded to the adult court, where they can be tried as adults and sentenced as adults if they have committed certain kinds of offenses. In Maryland, you've got researchers who are trying to define categories of delinquency such as the chronic offender. If a youngster is arrested four or five times, he is labeled a chronic offender, which means the system treats him differently from other youngsters. Some of those youngsters so classified can be youngsters who jumped a turnstile five consecutive times. This is one of the reasons contributing to a sharp increase in the number of minority youngsters in prison.

In California, it's age sixteen; in New York, it's thirteen. But other states are considering the same law. There has been, over the last two decades, a slow increase of about 3 percent a year of minorities in prisons. But over the last ten years, there has been a jump from 30 percent to 60 percent in California. There is great concern about this occurring all over the country.

If present trends continue, the jail populations in this country will change from 50 to 60 percent minority to 90 percent in less than five years. It is estimated that states are going to spend between $5 billion and $10 billion over that period for the construction of new jails.

That has been the history of the juvenile justice office. Again, those initiatives that have been funded have been diversion, prevention, restitution. The office spent $15.5 million going to forty municipal courts all over the country. If a youngster commits a property offense—and some money damages can be assessed—the court official will sit down with the youngster and the victim and work out a system to repay that person. All this is being carried out in nonurban areas. Seventy to 80 percent of the funds go to administration. Less than 3 percent gets into the victim's hands. Less than 3 percent are getting into the hands of the kids.

Eighty percent of the youngsters served by this program are non-minority. Because the courts have not or are not cooperating in most of these programs, less than half the money has been spent over the last two years. The same is true about the states. The office of juvenile justice is asking for $100 million, and Congress is about to pass it, at a time when the community anticrime program is getting ready to fold, with the rest of LEAA. The money is going to be spent for alternative education.

A research firm has suddenly determined that the best way to control and prevent juvenile delinquency is to fund the public school system, in order to prevent kids from dropping out of school. There is a correlation between dropouts, educational level, and delinquency. Based upon that correlation, they are going to put a lot of money into the school system.

In Denver, they are going to put $9 million into a program they call New Pride, that is supposed to be dealing with hard-core kids. The Colorado program depends upon professional social workers and counselors who interview kids—not the hard-core kids, as they say. They take them to the traditional counseling program. There are approximately eight to ten groups that are funded. To give you an example of who these groups are, they are the American Red Cross, the YMCAs, and a few other groups like that. The only money that has been identified for neighborhood groups is $2 million of the $100 million being appropriated; $2 million is supposed to be spent on neighborhood groups in what they are calling "capacity building." That is what they are going to have the various groups competing for, for the juvenile justice part.

Senator Birch Bayh, chairman of the committee, has released his bill; it's called the Serious Offender Act. This will continue the restitution programs: $19.5 million of what they call maintenance of effort will be spent on the arrest, trial and prosecution of kids who commit serious offenses. The courts and the police departments are going to receive some juvenile justice money to do that.

When the Law Enforcement Assistance Administration (LEAA) goes, the program will be under the Department of Health and Human Services or under the Justice Department. Those are the policies. Again, for dealing with delinquency prevention, there is very, very little; they think that the public school system is the answer.

I would encourage you to read the Serious Offender Act. The question is whether that policy speaks at all to the needs of the neighborhoods.

SISTER FATTAH: We can answer that right now. We had that policy back in the 1950s; it didn't work then.

SISTER FERRÉ: There was also a union of ACTION, and LEAA. What happened to it?

MR. WOODSON: That's a $15 million program under the Community Anti-Crime Program, a cooperative effort between ACTION and LEAA. First of all, in order to qualify for that program, a city has to be larger than 250,000. They have certain prescribed activities that they believe will control and prevent crime. They also prescribe whom you will cooperate with, under certain conditions, and what kind of approaches this program will take.

If you agree to apply this approach to the control and prevention of crime, and if you agree to develop these big coalitions to qualify, still most of the money is going to go to a prime sponsor with a track record of handling over $250,000 a year. What they are talking about is giving somebody like the Urban League or the NAACP $500,000, and they are to select up to ten programs that they can give $50,000 to, for crime prevention. If they give you $50,000 for an eighteen-month program, they're talking about you using 95 percent volunteers, because you can pay no salaries out of that, you can pay no rent, you can't pay electric bills out of it. It's really eaten up in the administrative costs of that umbrella agency. It was supposed to have been given to pay volunteer organizations, but they're telling you that you're going to have to stay volunteers.

MR. NIZAM FATAH: Can you imagine the New York City Transit Authority police receiving $500,000 to do counseling? They diverted about twenty-five of their kids to my program. We had no salaries at that time to do the counseling. When I found out that they had received the money for it, I shut it down. I shut it right down. I thought they were doing this as a humanitarian act, but I found out that they got the money and I got the problem.

SGT. HARGROVE: Their counselors were police officers they reassigned to their Youth Division (YD). Before, they used to give the youth either a YD report or a summons for those minor offenses. What they started doing with their new Youth Division was arresting them and then bringing them into the office and doing alleged counseling. When they used to make out the YD forms, they used to come to my unit in the police department and we used to do family counseling. It's one vicious circle. Now they lock them up, and they are a statistic.

They are attempting to do away with the youth division in the New York City Police Department. That's going to give the police officer on the street two options with a minor offense for a juvenile: either lock them up or let them go. In a high-crime community a youth is going to get locked up, and in a more affluent community he's going to be taken home. All of a sudden, you're going to see an increase in juvenile crime in New York City simply as a result of doing away with the youth division and of the diversion program that they have already started.

MR. WOODSON: This big juvenile crime wave will start when the funds hit the streets.

MR. NIZAM FATAH: In Brooklyn, there are 300 youth gangs or more. Actually, we know that there are more than that. Sergeant Hargrove deals with about 127. You know how big the New York City police force is—26,000. When you think about that, sometimes that doesn't sound like a lot, but it's larger than the armies of a lot of countries. How many officers do you have, Jimmy? Four, for the entire city. Only four cops in the street gang unit for New York City, because they told

Sergeant Hargrove last year that there were no youth gangs in New York.

SGT. HARGROVE: We declassify them on paper. If I go back tomorrow and I get out a report declassifying 127 youth gangs, there are no youth gangs in New York City. I could eliminate youth gangs in New York City tomorrow.

MR. WOODSON: We discussed Dr. Walter Miller's report, "Violence by Youth Gangs and Youth Groups as a Crime in Major American Cities," at our conference three years ago. We circulated a copy of his study and we analyzed it. We found that he visited twelve cities—by telephone—and interviewed 168 members of the criminal justice system, including one in New York.

SGT. HARGROVE: That was the commanding officer of the Youth Aid Division, who in three years never came to my Brooklyn unit.

MR. WOODSON: Those are the kinds of people that Walter Miller interviewed and then came out with projections about gangs. He didn't interview gang members or anyone who works on the street with gangs, nor did he interview anybody outside the juvenile justice system. Only social workers. He went on the "Today Show" with this information. He published an article in *Psychology Today*. When we discussed this, we presented it to the various groups and asked their reaction, since most of them represented the cities that Walter Miller mentioned. We pretty much put that whole issue to rest.

Walter Miller called me, after a *New York Times* article, to tell me it was just a preliminary study. But he was still talking about it on television and writing about it. A lot of the current policies regarding jails and what have you, are quoting the Miller study that was funded by the Office of Juvenile Justice and Delinquency Prevention as a position paper, upon which a policy was to be developed.

It's important for us to deal on the policy level as well as to deal with the concrete needs that you have on the street. A lot of the decisions about what happens on the street are going to be made by people who are listening to policy. They want to know what is a good policy direction to follow. That's why it's important that people who share a different point of view be consulted when these cities and others are formulating policies on juvenile justice. My hope is that they will begin to consult different kinds of people when they make these decisions. That's what this is all about.

I would like to end with a poem written by our resident poet, Earle C. Phillips.

As an observer
I see
Representing youth groups/gangs
From across the country and
    Puerto Rico
Old heads
With young leaders
Sitting tentatively/listening
To one another
As to the success
Of their program/sharing
What professionals
Need to know
To eliminate Gang Warfare.

I hear
Outcries of experience
From community people
Who not only
Realize the problem
But involve THEMSELVES
To take on more problems
As problem solvers
Of our youth
    KILLING OFF

Their future—and
The future of our cities . . .

RESULTS

House of Umoja
ICRY/Ching-A-Ling
Youth in Action
SEY YES—Who
Shake hands
Cross legs/meet
Eye-to-eye contact
With Washington/press
American Enterprise Institute
    at
Mayflower Hotel
    in
May
May/be
Hopefully
Start off the 80s
Not killing/destroying
But beating/conversationally
Some sense into America's
    Bureaucracy.

—EARLE C. PHILLIPS
House of Umoja

154

A NOTE ON THE BOOK

*The typeface used for the text of this book is
Times Roman, designed by Stanley Morison.
The type was set by
FotoTypesetters Incorporated, of Baltimore.
Thomson-Shore, Inc., of Dexter, Michigan, printed
and bound the book, using Warren's Olde Style paper.
The cover and format were designed by Pat Taylor.
The manuscript was edited by Ann Petty, and
by Claire Theune of the AEI Publications staff.*